GUITAR
Encyclopedia

GUITAR
Encyclopedia

BRIAN TARQUIN

ALLWORTH PRESS
NEW YORK

Allworth Press books may be purchased in bulk at special discounts for sales promotion, corporate gifts, fund-raising, or educational purposes. Special editions can also be created to specifications. For details, contact the Special Sales Department, Allworth Press, 307 West 36th Street, 11th Floor, New York, NY 10018 or info@skyhorsepublishing.com.

15 14 13 12 11 5 4 3 2 1

Published by Allworth Press, an imprint of Skyhorse Publishing, Inc.
307 West 36th Street, 11th Floor, New York, NY 10018.

Allworth Press® is a registered trademark of Skyhorse Publishing, Inc.®, a Delaware corporation.

www.allworth.com

Cover design by Mary Belibasakis
Cover and author photo by Erik Christian
Page composition/typography by Bsmart Publishing

Library of Congress Cataloging-in-Publication Data is available on file.

Print ISBN: 978-1-62153-406-8
Ebook ISBN: 978-1-62153-415-0

Printed in China

contents

Gary Hoey Playing Fender Strat

Foreword

foreword foreword
foreword foreword

started playing guitar in 1974 when I was fourteen. My first electric was a hand-me-down Sears-catalog guitar named Norma, a forty-dollar beauty—she was the only girl my mom let me take to my room. Within a year I was obsessed with the electric guitar. I dreamed of getting a real pro guitar and had my eyes on a Black Gibson Les Paul Standard because "It" was on the cover of the Jeff Beck album *Blow By Blow*. I took the album to my local music store and said, "I want this guitar." I still have it. Since then I've owned Gibson, Fender, B. C. Rich, Hamer, Charvel, Ibanez, PRS, Jackson, ESP, and Rickenbacker and even built a few from kits. I thought they all were the best thing I'd ever played at the time, and then the love would fade away and I would be on the hunt for my next favorite sound.

I taught guitar for years, and I could not recall some of my students' names, but I could recall the guitar they played. I used to buy guitars because my heroes played them, and I realized the sound is in your hands. It's how you let the instrument breathe that makes it sing, but having the right guitar can really make it sing. I've been playing Strats since 1996, and it's the sound I hear in my head; players have to find the sound in their head and a guitar that feels good in their hands.

A Fender Strat has sexy curves that hug your body. Buddy Holly made the Fender Strat famous with the song "Peggy Sue," but look at what has been done with the same exact instrument for almost sixty years. The first time I heard Jimi Hendrix play a Fender Stratocaster I heard another dimension in sound—Jimi and Stevie Ray Vaughan stop me dead in my tracks.

A Gibson Les Paul is like a chunk of a tree that you can beat on and it doesn't move. Some of my favorite Gibson players are Jimmy Page, Slash, and Ted Nugent; Nugent played a hollow body and made the feedback and art form. Duane Allman and Gary Moore were also big for me. A Jackson makes you want to crank to ten and play heavy metal.

Like the late Randy Rhoads and his guitars (most notably a custom Gibson Les Paul and a Polka Dot Flying V), there are as many styles of electric guitars as there are personalities, and there are certain guitarists we associate with them. Mark Knopfler for the out-of-phase Strat sound, Keith Richards with the Telecaster, The Beatles with the Rickenbacker, Angus Young with the Gibson SG, and Jimmy Page with the Les Paul. The beautiful thing about an electric guitar is from the first five minutes you play it you can fall in love just by the way the neck feels in your hands or the sound when you hit that first power chord. If it doesn't pass that test, then it's back to the rack it goes.

If it wasn't for the electric guitar there would be no dive bombs, volume swells, pinch harmonics, feedback, or effects pedals, and what would we do with our feet? We would all hear a little better, but it's all worth it. Right?

— Gary Hoey, guitarist, producer

Introduction

introduction introduction introduction
introduction introduction

n the rural south of pre-1930, it was not uncommon to get a length of bailing wire, hammer two nails in a board, and string up a "diddley bow" that could be played with a piece of metal used as a slide. This one-string "guitar" with its droning atonal musicality was an early precursor to the slide guitar playing of Charlie Patton, Robert Johnson, and other masters who came to dominate blues music. And it was the blues guitar music that begat fifty years of rock 'n' roll, raising the art form to a high level powered by the enthusiasm of baby-boom kids across the world.

The painter has his palette and brushes of all types, the mechanic has his tools, and the guitar player has his own specialized instruments: six or twelve strings, different scale lengths, numerous design and construction techniques, different types of wood and other materials, as well as acoustic or electric amplification. Even within the confines of type, the electric guitar is differentiated by various pickup designs, styles, and layouts, by tremolo and other string location systems, by body shapes, and by weight, length, height, width, and any of a thousand other variables. Indeed, the diversity is endless, and variety of available instruments enhances the experience of playing the guitar.

This encyclopedia documents the richness of the guitar in all its varieties and traces the history and design evolution of the instrument over the years and in response to player needs. The focus is not only the instrument, but also the great minds behind the guitar's development as it grew to become the number-one instrument in popular music. Perusing the pages, several themes emerge: Orville, Leo, and Les were way out front as thinkers on guitar design; history is important, but old guitars aren't necessarily better than modern ones; great tone is subjective and can be found in many instruments; and, finally, playing feel directly impacts the musician's approach.

It is that all-important "feel" that drives the great variety of instruments represented here and that operates as an element in all of the brands, styles, and designs of guitars represented here. Indeed, it is the playing feel that led the great Bo Diddley, who took his stage name from the diddley bow, to create his unique "shave-and-a-haircut-two-bits" rhythm sound that is at once familiar to all of those baby-boom rockers from over the years.

— Eric Shoaf, *Vintage Guitar Magazine*

◄ Vintage Guitar *Writer Eric Shoaf with Gibson L7*

Brian Tarquin Handmade Strat Body Circa 1989

Steve Vai with the JEM

CHAPTER 1

Guitar Mojo

The electric guitar has the kind of mojo and swagger that Marlon Brando possessed in the film *The Wild One* and reverberates such tonal awe as the names of the infamous gunslingers in the American Old West. It was born out the mahoganies, ashes, and maples grown tall in the great American forests themselves. These magnificently carved, curvacious instruments contain the true DNA of our American music culture of the twentieth century. Nothing more sacred and holy, except for the Crucifix, can pass through the fingers of guitarists to create such alluring and passionate tones. However, it starts with the forgotten heroes who created such tone monsters, the luthiers, whose whole origin stretches back to the medieval times. The word itself takes its roots from the French word "*luth*," which means lute, the craft of making string instruments. Without Orville Gibson, Leo Fender, Les Paul, Adolph Rickenbacker, and men of like minds, there would be no sexy double cutaway modern guitars or beautiful 7-string monsters that Steve Vai commanded on stage with prowess.

These men labored in their shops to produce the perfect tools that created that distinct sound we call the guitar and should be acknowledged for their contribution to music and for furthering the evolution of the guitar.

Nothing is more satisfying than working with wood and creating a musical instrument, if for no other reason than for the satisfaction of conquering that blank piece of ash and forming it into something that can make musical notes. I know because in my early years I took on this difficult task of guitar building, first in woodshop classes in high school and then later in my own workshop in my early twenties. It was an incredible experience using various tools to form the guitar body and to see how it all took shape through the various stages of building. In those days it was hard to actually buy wood blanks to cut the bodies out of, so I would glue two pieces of wood together side by side with wood dowels and clamp them in place for twenty-four hours for the glue to dry. We next went to planing the wood level, cutting the actual rough shape of the guitar, and then routing out the various cavities; from there the task was refining the wood.

The smell of freshly cut wood and sawdust was the scent of creativity working overtime, and visualizing the piece of wood taking shape and eventually playing guitar tones was enough incentive to see the project through to the end. My point is this: in today's corporate mass manufacturing world, how easy it is to forget the origins of the guitar when you're standing in Guitar Center staring at one of those 6-string beauties and all you want to do is cut a good deal with the sales guy and out the store you go! A quote from the father of Epiphone Guitars, Epi Stathopoulo, was, "Good musical instruments do not just happen." How true that is. Just remember that the next time you go into your local music store and pick up that killer guitar.

Early Roots

There is no other instrument in the history of the world that had such a huge musical and cultural impact as the birth of the electric guitar in the twentieth century. Sure, the roots of this peculiar stringed instrument go back to the ancient times of the Romans, who developed a four-string version called the *oud*. Later the Spanish developed the *vihuela,* or *viola da mano,* which basically combined the lute and the oud. But it wasn't until the 1920s with the advent of the phonograph and the radio that the guitar got a real volume boost. In 1928, the American company Stromberg-Voisinet introduced the first commercial electric guitar, called the Stromberg Electro. Later the company changed its name to Kay Musical Instrument Company and continued making guitars up until the '60s. During the same period, the Vega Company, based in Boston, became known for its electric banjos, which included a small amplifier. But the real developer of the electric guitar was the company Ro-Pat-In, which later became Rickenbacker, formed in the early 1930s. Interestingly, the company's success laid in its pickup design and its marketing strategy, aimed directly to, believe it or not, Hawaiian guitarists.

Starting in 1931, the Los Angeles company National, founded by John Dopyera and George Beauchamp, was one of the first to embrace a shift in manufacturing from acoustic to electric instruments. Later in the thirties, National merged with another one of Dopyera's companies to form National-Dobro and ventured out to Hawaiian guitars, Electric lap steels, and mandolins, which were branded under three different companies, National, Dobro, and Supro.

Ironically, one of the great American guitar manufacturers, Epiphone, started its roots in the Greek mountains in Kastania. Epaminondas (Epi) Stathopoulo was the son of a mandolin luthier, Anastasios, who emigrated to the United States with

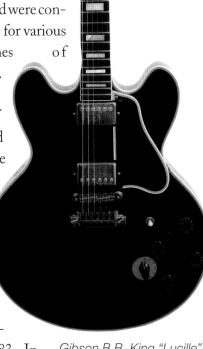

his family in the early twentieth century. Like many immigrants at the time, Epi's father, Anastasios, lived on the Lower East Side of Manhattan and opened up a musical repair shop on the ground floor, with the family living above the shop. By the mid-1930s Epiphone moved its showroom to midtown Manhattan and became one of the most well-known and respected guitar builders in the industry. It managed to keep Gibson on its toes.

Last but not least is the company that lagged behind all of the others but became the most influential guitar builder in the world, Gibson. It was in 1938 that Gibson really set the bar with the ES-150, which was a much smaller guitar scale than what we are used to today, only 16 inches wide. But what made this guitar such a pioneer was the man who played it, none other than the legendary Charlie Christian. At the time, the guitar only had a single bar pickup by the neck and was marketed with a little amp. What makes this so important is that Charlie Christian went on to make this particular guitar famous in Benny Goodman's swing band. He was the first to take single note solos on the guitar and actually be heard over all of those horns and strings, a major hallmark at the time when most popular music was swing-

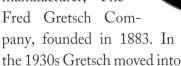
John Lennon Epiphone "Revolution" Guitar

band oriented. Charlie's playing reached much further than jazz, and in 1990 he was inducted into the Rock and Roll Hall of Fame. He paved the way for later guitarists such as B.B. King, Chuck Berry, and Jimi Hendrix.

Post-War

In 1947 Nathan Daniel founded the Danelectro Company, which produced amplifiers for Sears & Roebuck and Montgomery Ward and were contracted to make guitars for various stores under the names of Silvertone and Airline. In 1954 it went on to produce its own line of solid body guitars and amplifiers. But there was a much more established company in Brooklyn, New York, that was both a distributor and drum manufacturer, The Fred Gretsch Company, founded in 1883. In the 1930s Gretsch moved into

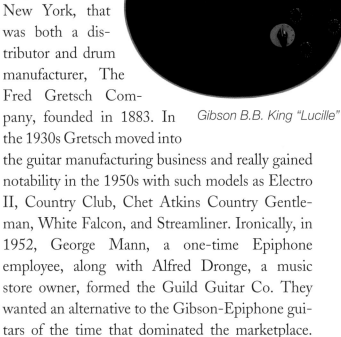
Gibson B.B. King "Lucille"

the guitar manufacturing business and really gained notability in the 1950s with such models as Electro II, Country Club, Chet Atkins Country Gentleman, White Falcon, and Streamliner. Ironically, in 1952, George Mann, a one-time Epiphone employee, along with Alfred Dronge, a music store owner, formed the Guild Guitar Co. They wanted an alternative to the Gibson-Epiphone guitars of the time that dominated the marketplace.

From their New York City midtown factory they launched such classics as Stratford 375, Stuart 500, X-550, and Manhattan X-175B. But it was in Fullerton, California, where a new solid body guitar was born from a man who had his own radio repair shop, Leo Fender. As the '50s developed, big bands fell out of style and transitioned over to smaller combo groups playing boogie-woogie and Western swing, hence the birth of the Esquire, a single pickup Tele and the double pickup Telecaster and Broadcaster. In 1951, Leo introduced the new radical four-string solid body Precision Bass. Then in 1954 the revolution occurred! The birth of the iconic Stratocaster, the guitar that took over rock 'n' roll and inevitably changed the sound of music forever in the hands of Hendrix a decade later!

Modern Age

It wasn't until after Vietnam and Watergate, when everything looked hopelessly locked into the old established guitar makers, that a breath of fresh air blew in from the East! Many Japanese guitar manufacturers in the '60s first started out making copies of guitars from well-known U.S. guitar builders like Fender and Gibson, but after debilitating lawsuits, they went on to design their own styles, with Ibanez leading the way.

Fender Strat Relic

Who can forget George Benson shredding on his signature series GB10 that was enough for him to give up playing his Gibson L-5? One of its all-time prominent designs was the Iceman, which launched in 1975 and was given great exposure with endorsees like Steve Miller and Kiss guitarist Paul Stanley. But their tour de force series was the Steve Vai JEM guitar equipped with "monkey grip," Edge whammy bar, and DiMarzio pickups. In the '80s Ibanez made certain to endorse every American shredder to its line of guitars, musicians like Joe Satriani, Paul Gilbert, John Petrucci, and others, which was a great PR move for the brand.

ESP (Electric Sound Products) located in Tokyo, Japan, also found similar success in the '80s. Founded in 1976, ESP started out as a

Ibanez Black Artist Guitar

replacement parts company supplying necks and bodies to other manufacturers such as Kramer, Robin, and Schecter. Following suit with Ibanez, ESP landed every available heavy metal guitarist possible with the likes of George Lynch, James Hetfield, Kirk Hammett, and Dave Mustaine for propaganda ads that spilled out to the guitar magazines of the time.

One of the most soaring successes of the '80s was the manufacturer of Kramer guitars. Starting out as a quirky builder of aluminum-neck guitars and basses, Kramer turned into an iconic guitar builder for one of the greatest guitarists in history, Eddie Van Halen. As it turns out, all they needed was to get the Van Halen endorsement and add an obscure tremolo designer to the mix that guaranteed that strings would not go out of tune no matter how hard you'd hit the Floyd Rose whammy bar. All the stars were aligned, and in 1983 they came out with their flagship model, Baretta, which was a faithful re-creation of Eddie's guitar with the one bridge angled pickup, one volume knob (no treble knob), Floyd Rose tremolo, pointy headstock, and even on some models an exact red,

Kramer USA Eddie Van Halen Guitar

white, and black paint job on the body. The die had been cast—like thousands of others I ran to the nearest store and bought one from Sam Ash on 48th Street! I should add that Kramer was the first guitar manufacturer who offered the new Floyd Rose–designed locking tremolo system at the time. Later, Ibanez would design its own locking tremolo system and offer it on certain models; however,

Kramer was very advanced for the period. As a note, I had gone around a year before in 1982 to see how much it would cost to buy and install a Floyd Rose system on my current Ibanez Blazer II; the price was exorbitant. I think the tremolo cost $300 itself, and it cost the same amount to install. Why bother, when a year later you could get a new Kramer model preinstalled with a Floyd Rose for the same price?

Of course, what followed was a real catch-up with all of the guitar manufacturers working to get with the new program of the Strat design with a locking tremolo. So companies like Jackson, Charvel, Washburn, Yamaha, Gibson, Fender, and the like all devoted time to new designs to win the young generation of budding guitarists.

Randy Rhoads Polka Dot Flying V

Then there was Paul Reed Smith, the third-largest guitar manufacturer today behind Gibson and Fender. Like many of the luthiers throughout history we see PRS first taking up shop at his parents' house, but eventually moving into his own larger workshop. The important fact here is he was able to connect to famous players, as we've seen in other manufacturers. Fortunately, he was able to do it early on, making his first guitars for Ted Nugent, Peter Frampton, and Al Di Meola. However, it was his association with one of the finest guitarists of our generation, Carlos Santana, that really proved to be his turning point. Santana would give him the credibility he needed for the years to come with his struggle to establish the PRS brand.

You can't mention modern guitars without noting the Roland guitar synth series. Starting out in 1972 in Osaka, Japan, the company closely associated with midi instruments, keyboards, and beat boxes, also led the way in guitar synthesis. One of the great-looking Jedson guitars is the Roland G-707 equipped with real strings, alder body, maple neck, rosewood fingerboard, tremolo bar, and reverse headstock. Afterward Roland went into making pickups including the special GK-2A divided pickup. I had a GK-2A series pickup I installed on an old Tele that connected to the synth module via cable, which a GK 13-pin sounded very good and tracked surprisingly well, and which I took to record with in London during my solo artist days on Instinct Records. Listen, if you are a guitarist and are used to the fingering and voicings of the guitar, it is much more natural to play keyboard sounds on the guitar. It's all how you use it in conjunction with the song. Roland really had this guitar synth market all sewn up for themselves, with the small exception of Casio, which was an inferior product, and the SynthAxe, which was on the other end of the spectrum—extremely expensive and very complicated to operate.

The manufacturers and players may change through the history of the guitar, but the real basics will always be present: playability and innovation. From our guitar inventor forefathers who came from long-ago Greece to the most modern American guitar maker, it's all about the art of the guitar. Through its beautiful shapes, curves, angles, and graphic texture paints, they produce the most outrageous sounds and tones. As Jimi Hendrix once stated, "Technically, I am not a guitar player, all I play is truth and emotion," and that's all we can expect from the guitar— truth and emotion!

Paul Reed Smith Double Cutaway

Brian Tarquin with Fender Paisley Tele Equipped with Roland GK-2A Synth Pickup Instinct Records Promo Shot

CHAPTER 2

Epaminondas ("Epi") Stathopoulo

The history of Epiphone guitars lies in a rich and fascinating culture that dates back to the nineteenth-century Ottoman Empire. It all started in 1873 in Smyrna (now called Izmir), Turkey, with Anastasios Stathopoulo, a Greek luthier of fiddles, bouzoukis, and the oud, which is the Middle Eastern lute. Anastasios learned his trade and knowledge of tonewoods from his father, Kostantinos, and by 1890 he had gained a reputation as a talented luthier and eventually opened up his own shop manufacturing musical instruments. Then in 1893 the prodigal son was born, Epaminondas, who was followed by other children, Alex, Minnie, Orpheus, and Frixo. As fate would have it, the imposing taxes by the Ottoman Empire on Greek immigrants forced Anastasios to take his family, like so many other Europeans at the time, to America, the promised land. So, at age forty Anastasios boards a ship with his family in tow and voyages to Ellis Island. Like so many immigrants in 1903, the Stathopoulo family settles in the Lower East Side of Manhattan, where Anastasios starts up his reputation as an instrument builder. Records show that Anastasios filed for his only patent in 1909 for a mandolin with a rounded bowl-style back.

Epaminondas, known as "Epi," quickly became Americanized and went on to attend Columbia University. Through his life Epi apprenticed with his father in instrument making and at age twenty-two found himself in charge of the family business when his father passed away. Having a keen sense of marketing, Epi replaced his father's old instrument label with a new one called "The House of Stathopoulo, Quality Instruments Since 1873" to modernize the family business. With the passing of his mother in 1923, Epi took full control of the business and launched a Recording line of banjos. He also stopped manufacturing old

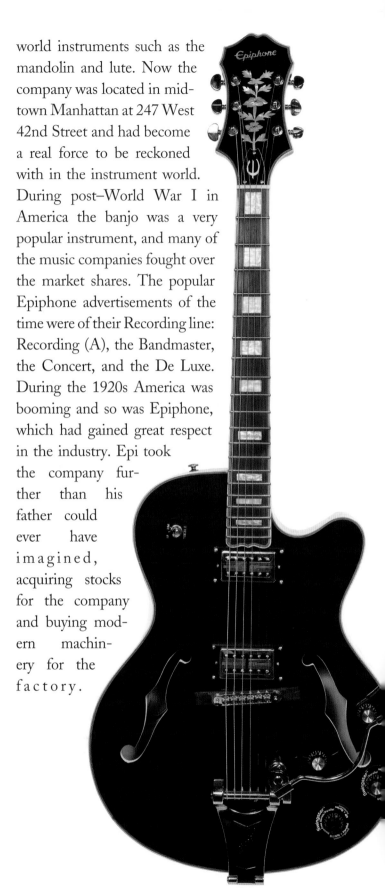

world instruments such as the mandolin and lute. Now the company was located in midtown Manhattan at 247 West 42nd Street and had become a real force to be reckoned with in the instrument world. During post–World War I in America the banjo was a very popular instrument, and many of the music companies fought over the market shares. The popular Epiphone advertisements of the time were of their Recording line: Recording (A), the Bandmaster, the Concert, and the De Luxe. During the 1920s America was booming and so was Epiphone, which had gained great respect in the industry. Epi took the company further than his father could ever have imagined, acquiring stocks for the company and buying modern machinery for the factory.

Epiphone Emperor Swingster Guitar

Epiphone Joe Pass Signature Guitar

This is the time period where Epi changed the name of the company to Epiphone, a reference to the Greek word meaning sound: phone. He even released a statement to the trade publications at the time stating, "The new policy of business and all interest will be devoted to the production of banjos, tenor banjos, banjo mandolins, banjo guitars, and banjo ukuleles under the registered trademark name of 'Epiphone.'" Epiphone acquired the Farovan Company instrument plant in Long Island and kept most of its skilled employees to achieve improvements of quality and production. Now don't think Epi was just a behind-the-desk marketing CEO type; he was a great designer in his own right, in fact he filed a patent for a popular banjo design early on in the company's history.

Epiphone's biggest rival at the time was Gibson guitars in Kalamazoo, Michigan. As the inventors of the archtop guitar and having great success with the L-5, Gibson was at the top of its game in the 1920s. But Epiphone developed an answer: the Masterbilt series that included the De Luxe,

Epiphone Les Paul Plus Top Pro/FX Model

Broadway, and the Triumph, which boasted carved spruce tops, flame curly maple backs, large F holes, and ornate black and white bindings. This developed into a huge guitar war between Gibson and Epiphone through the next decade, where each of the companies tried to outdo the other with new guitar designs. During the 1930s Gibson released the king-size Super 400, and then Epiphone released the Emperor, having a wider body, then the De Luxe, Broadway, and Triumph models, making them wider than Gibson's existing archtops. Epiphone became one of the greatest guitar manufacturers by 1935 and even ventured into exporting their instruments through the UK company Handcraft, Ltd. By this time, they opened a new showroom on 14th Street, which became a hangout spot for New York musicians like Les Paul and Harry Volpe, who would jam there on Saturday afternoons. Epi also dove into manufacturing electric steel guitars after seeing the great success that Rickenbacker had with their models. So in the mid-1930s they introduced the Electraphone, which featured a master pickup that had individual, adjustable pole pieces.

But like many businesses at the time, everything changed when World War II broke out. The company's biggest loss was the man himself, Epi Stathopoulo, who died of leukemia in 1943. The remaining brothers argued on the company's direction and moved the factory out of New York to Philadelphia, which affected craftsmanship greatly when many of the workers left the company to stay in New York. What resulted was a lack of vision and innovation that disappeared after Epi's death. So it was inevitable that its archrival, Gibson, would wind up buying the company for a measly $20K in 1957 and Epiphone would become Gibson's solution for

Epiphone Double Neck Model 1275

Epiphone Jack Cassidy Bass Model

smaller, less profitable dealers to sell around the country. It was during the 1960s "British Invasion" when the Epiphone guitars became a real classic. They appeared in the hands of Keith Richards and Brian Jones of The Rolling Stones, John Lennon and Paul McCartney of The Beatles, and Dave Davies of The Kinks. In fact, in the year 1961 Epiphone sold 3,798 instruments, which was the same year that they introduced the Casino. In between 1961 to 1965, Epiphone enjoyed a boom in profits, up fivefold. The next two decades would prove difficult for Epiphone to keep afloat, especially when Ecuadorian ECL Corporation, a beer company, bought Gibson and the emergence of foreign-made guitars surged. But the renaissance of the company really took place in the 1990s when Epiphone took back their heritage and rereleased the Casino, Riviera, Sorrento, and Rivoli bass. From that point forward to the present, Epiphone really showed they still made some of the greatest instruments. I remember when Zakk Wylde told me that he could take his model off the shelf whether it was a Gibson or Epiphone and play it, to him there was no difference in quality; and I can attest to that!

Epiphone Zakk Wylde Les Paul Model

Epiphone Nikki Sixx Blackbird Model

Epiphone 1963 Firebird Reissue

Epiphone Emperor Regent Model

Epiphone ES-175 Reissue

Epiphone 1958 Korina Explorer Reissue

Epiphone 1961 Casino Tremotone

Epiphone 1966 Worn Wilshire

Epiphone Airscreamer

Epiphone Alleykat

Epiphone Annihilation

Epiphone Apparition

Epiphone Broadway

Epaminondas ("Epi") Stathopoulo • **31**

Epiphone Bob Marley Les Paul Special

Epiphone Zakk Wylde Graveyard Model

Epiphone Dwight Trash Model Jackpot White

Epiphone Zenith Robot

Epiphone Emperor
Swingster

*Epiphone Emily the
Strange G-310*

*Epiphone Zakk Wylde
Coffin Model*

Epiphone Dot Royale

Epiphone 1961
Casino Model

Epiphone ES-295 Model

*Epiphone ES-339
Pro Model*

CHAPTER 3

Leo Fender

Leo Fender Leo Fender
Leo Fender Leo Fender

Who would think the guitar that changed the world and sparked the six-string revolution in the 1960s was born out of a radio repair shop in Fullerton, California. To understand the origins of the electric guitar, you have to know the times in which it was created. In the 1930s, Hawaiian lap steel guitars were in vogue; many instrument manufacturers like Rickenbacker on the West Coast were producing these models. Leo was no different, and he dove into a partnership with Clayton Orr "Doc" Kauffman, who had worked at Rickenbacker making lap steel guitars. The partnership was called "K & F Manufacturing Corporation" in 1945. But this was a short-lived partnership, and the two split in 1946; Leo went on to form Fender Electric Instrument Co. in 1947. Although he continued to produce lap steel guitars, he started to tinker with the idea of a solid body, to reduce feedback when amplified. Manufacturers like Gibson, Rickenbacker, National, and Epiphone all made various types of hollow body guitars for years, but there was a desire from musicians to have a solid body guitar—after all a man named Lester William Polsfuss (Les Paul) was doing this in New York. By 1950 Leo had his first solid body guitar in production, the Esquire, later the Broad-caster, and ultimately the Telecaster. It was just a solid slab of ash with a single cutaway and a bolt-on maple neck, as basic as it gets. It had three adjustable saddles, two pickups, neck position, and a slanted bridge position mounted in a steel plate. Simple, yet perfect to go into mass production.

As with everything new, the Esquire proved to be a tough sale at first, especially when it was introduced at the 1950 musical instrument trade show in Chicago. Fender was one of the first manufacturers to use form and function to make practical guitars so they could be easily assembled and affordably priced for the end user. One of the first guitarists to appreciate the Esquire was Jimmy Bryant, who had a jazz/country style and who played with pedal steel guitarist Speedy West. The duo appeared on many TV shows at the time and played on recordings with Tex Williams and Tennes-see Ernie Ford. It was Western swing music that first featured the electric guitar and pedal steel guitar in Texas dance halls in the 1940s. Hard work paid off for Leo because by the mid-1950s he

Fender Tele Reissue

Fender Tele Thinline Reissue

expanded the factory in new buildings over a 3.5-acre lot in Fullerton.

Then in 1954 it happened, the guitar that would change rock 'n' roll forever and give the beautiful sound of dive-bombs, the Stratocaster, was born! This gorgeous, sleek beauty featured a tremolo bar for all sorts of pitch effects, six bridge saddles, three single-coil pickups, pick guard, and a new recessed input jack on the face of the body. Everything about the Strat was new and advanced, yet such a classic that it stays with us to this day. Again like the Esquire, dealers were reluctant to carry it, being very discouraged with the tremolo, some even stating, "Who needs it?" Well, they just would have to wait a decade to see who needed it. Can you say "Are You Experienced" Jimi Hendrix?

By the late 1950s Leo wanted to outdo his Strat creation so he designed the Jazzmaster, which was a much flashier guitar at the time. It had a separate rosewood fin-gerboard glued on top of the maple neck, a new floating tremolo system, a gold pick guard made from aluminum, slider selector switchers, unique body shape, and an enlarged headstock. The one downside of the gui-tar was those large unshielded

Fender Tele Custom Reissue

Fender Jazzmaster Reissue

pickups, which picked up a lot of hum and noise on stage and in the studio. But in spite of the pickups, the Jazzmaster remained on top of the Fender catalog all the way until the 1980s. The early 1960s saw new models like the Jaguar and the Mustang come into fruition at Fender. The Jaguar was an improved Jazzmaster with better-shielded pickups and a shorter scale, shorter than the usual Fender neck scale. The Mustang on the other hand was a lower-priced student guitar that again had the tremolo system, contoured body, complete with two single pickups.

By the time CBS purchased the company for $13 million in 1965, Fender had firmly established itself as the top guitar manufacturer in America. It made history for the time as the highest purchase price for a single music manufacturer. So ended an era of guitar building and ushered in a new period of mass manufacturing. Two generations collided: the old Fender craftsmen who had no formal training, building each guitar by hand, and the new college engineers who believed in the bottom dollar of profits from mass production. As with many large companies that acquired new businesses, CBS poured money into Fender to achieve guitar manufacturing on a large scale. So in the beginning, profits and sales were indeed up, but inevitably the CBS years were looked on as an unsettling time, with mixed reviews on their products when they reached the 1970s. Inevitably another sale was eminent. In 1985 William Schultz, then company president, with a group of employees and investors, purchased Fender from CBS. This would usher an entire era of rebirth for Fender, which by the mid-1980s had become unfavorable to

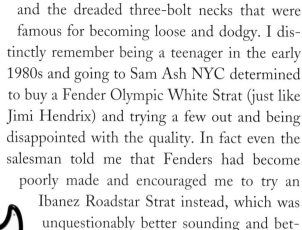

Fender Geddy Lee Jazz Bass Model

Fender Pawn Shop 1972

many guitar buyers, with cheaply made Strats and the dreaded three-bolt necks that were famous for becoming loose and dodgy. I distinctly remember being a teenager in the early 1980s and going to Sam Ash NYC determined to buy a Fender Olympic White Strat (just like Jimi Hendrix) and trying a few out and being disappointed with the quality. In fact even the salesman told me that Fenders had become poorly made and encouraged me to try an Ibanez Roadstar Strat instead, which was unquestionably better sounding and better made than the current Fenders. So sorry, Jimi—I bought the Ibanez for so many reasons and never looked back. This was the same period when the explosion of Strat copies came on the guitar scene, like Jackson, Charvel, Ibanez, ESP, Kramer, and Schecter. These were companies that took the basic design of the Fender Strat, gave it custom features like the locking tremolo system, humbucker pickups, and ornate paint jobs. But in 1987 Fender found a new place in the market when they opened up the Fender Custom Shop and started building their Artist Signature Series; players like Jeff Beck, Eric Clapton, James Burton, Stevie Ray Vaughan, Will Ray, Danny Gatton, and of course the 1990's Jimi Hendrix. Hence, Fender is still with us and has had a long and assorted history, but has managed to remain a dominant force in the industry, while acquiring many other guitar manufacturers that were once their rivals, like Charvel, Jackson, Guild, Gretsch, and even Kaman Music Corp., which owns Ovation and Hamer. Not bad for a guy who started out repairing radios in Fullerton, California.

FENDER LUTHIER LARRY BROOKS

One of my good friends happens to be a renowned guitar builder with oodles of knowledge, Larry Brooks, the man! He has an incredible knowledge of guitars and years of experience of intricate building. I met Larry when he was head of Artist Relations at Seymour Duncan pickups in Santa Barbara. Larry is a great guy, along with his wife, Karen. So it was a pleasure to drive down from L.A. back in the day to get my guitars set up by Larry. The wonderful stories he had of Eric Clapton and how he achieved the unreal smoothness on Eric's maple neck. When I first started brainstorming this book, Larry was the first to come to mind to interview and share his knowledge with others.

Can you give us a little background on yourself and how you got started with guitar building and making custom guitars?

I knew at a young age that I wanted to be a part of music. It was then that I heard Bill Haley and the Comets, and I knew from that point on the guitar and singing was what I wanted to do, and I've been playing guitar and singing ever since. I was on the road for a few years and was having trouble finding a guitar that really met my needs. It was at that point I began to explore the mechanics of guitar. This was in 1967. My problem was that the guitars available, at that time, were either too heavy, or too awkward, the necks were either too thick, or too flat, and so on and so on. I started to buy garage sale guitars, broken guitars. I felt they were bad anyway, and I could not make them any worse. After a year or so I started to sell the ones I had worked on, made enough money to buy a few tools and the rest is history. I stopped playing full time, started building and repairing. I got a job at a music store. Started selling, playing, repairing,

and building, and I have never stopped custom building, even while working at the top guitar manufacturing company in the world. My last position was master builder for artist relations at the Fender Custom shop. There I was lucky enough to build for the top guitar players in the world today. While there I built about 235 guitars, all of which were to the specific needs of each player.

Fender Eric Clapton Signature Model

It seems that in the world of CNC manufacturing, the art of the guitar luthier is lost. How did you come up with the unique designs and what makes your guitars so different?

CNC machines, or guitar cookie cutting as I call it, has really hurt every custom guitar builder, as well as all custom instrument builders. Why would a guitarist buy a custom-made guitar when he can buy a cookie-cut guitar for so much less and just change the parts to whatever he needs! Like most

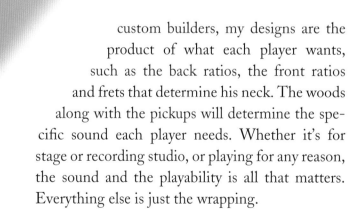

custom builders, my designs are the product of what each player wants, such as the back ratios, the front ratios and frets that determine his neck. The woods along with the pickups will determine the specific sound each player needs. Whether it's for stage or recording studio, or playing for any reason, the sound and the playability is all that matters. Everything else is just the wrapping.

Fender Larry Brooks Custom Shop for Brian Tarquin Circa 2002

Can you tell us how it was making guitars for Clapton, Stevie Ray Vaughan, and Kurt Cobain?

Building for Eric Clapton was a real challenge! He was looking for a Strat that was exactly like his favorite and most famous Fender Strat. But it was so different from other 1957 Strats that I had to play it before I could even try to match it. So with my road kit and a blank guitar neck, Fender flew me to New York where he was playing, so I could play the original "Blackie" Strat. It was really a different neck, it had a very sharp V shape; instead of the V stopping at around the 5th fret, it went all the way to the 10th fret. That's why all other Strats felt so different to Eric. I took the info back to my hotel room, and there I shaped what would become the production "Clapton Blackie." Eric was so pleased with the guitar that he gave Fender the go-ahead to build his signature Strat, as long as they built it to the neck shape specs I had built for him.

Kurt Cobain had called Fender and wanted to know if they would be interested in building a custom guitar based off two Fenders that he really liked. They came to me and asked if I would give it a try. So off I went to meet with Kurt. The guitar he wanted built was a marriage of two Fender guitars, a Jaguar and a Mustang. After a few sketches we came up with a design that he really liked, and the "Jag-Stang" was born!

I had started to work on the Stevie Ray Vaughan Signature model when he tragically was killed in a helicopter accident. Fender decided to postpone building the SRV signature Strat. They did not want anyone to think that they were trying to capitalize on such a tragedy. It was about a month later, and I was given the go-ahead to complete the work, so they could start work on its production. The Strat has a three-tone sunburst, a left-hand vintage vibrato, a 1962 style neck and the new single coil pickups I wound, which are now called the "Texas Special."

Fender Kurt Cobain Jaguar Signature Model

Fender Kurt Cobain Mustang Signature Model

Can you take us through your process of building from choosing the right wood to the paint finishing?

The steps in building any custom guitar are the same. The first step, whether it's an acoustic guitar, a nylon string classical guitar, a solid body guitar or an arched top jazz guitar, is to obtain all of the wood. This includes the wood for the neck, fretboard and body. For acoustic guitars you need separate pieces of wood for the top, the back, and the sides. Next, you will need to get fret wire for the neck, tuning keys, and any electronic components, such as pickups, potentiometers (these are for volume and tone controls), and in some cases an onboard preamp.

Next is to decide on the finish. This can be one of the trickiest parts. You need to know whether you're going to put on a clear natural finish, stained finish, or a color finish. Then come the clear coats. The final step is to decide the type of paint you are going to use, whether it's enamel, nitrocellulose lacquer, or polyurethane. Painting is one of the most frustrating procedures in all of custom guitar building. There are so many variables, the worst of which are dust, humidity, and temperature. If these can be eliminated, you will have a start in obtaining a desired good-looking finish. After all these years of finishing custom guitars, I finally have been able to break the finishing down to no fewer than twenty-eight frustrating steps, starting with the sanding of the wood all the way to the last steps, buffing and polishing.

Custom building has always been and always will be my lifelong passion. I have learned along the way that hard work and dedication are very important, but the single most important ingredient is patience! Patience while learning the many techniques, patience with your time, and the hardest one of all to master is patience with yourself!

There always seems to be a debate about the finishes nitro vs. poly. What is the difference and how does it affect the tone of the instrument?

The materials used in finishing the guitar will have a big impact on its overall tone and sustain. It does not matter whether it's a solid body or an acoustic. There are two basic paints being used on guitars. Polyurethane and nitrocellulose lacquer. Polyurethane will give you a durable and glossy finish; however, I prefer to use lacquer. It not only allows the body to retain its tone quality, but it will also produce a much higher gloss. I call it the "wet look." The biggest downfall is that lacquer, as it ages, has a history of cracking and peeling. It also is much easier to dent and chip more so than polyurethane finishes. Now about polyurethane finishes. A polyurethane finish tends to darken and muffle the sound and inhibit sustain. It does this because it is a much heavier paint. But no matter what type of material is being used it's important to coat or spray the least amount of paint you can get away with and still get a good-looking finish.

Fender Deluxe Precision Bass

Do you wind your own pickups or use a third party and how important are the electronics in your guitars?

Most of the time I use my own "house wound" custom pickups, then I can combine the pickups with the chosen wood to create the final tone and color of the guitar sound. At this point I have to say (very maddening to me), I use the bobbins from other manufacturers pickups. If I custom make and complete a pickup myself, for my own guitars, there will be legal ramifications from pickup manufacturers. I cannot make pickups that they patent without their permission . . . so, I completely disassemble pickups, working or not, and rebuild them to my specification. Pickups are a big challenge for me because they are the very heart of the electric guitar, and like all guitarists I'm on that lifelong journey! Searching for that ever-elusive *perfect tone*.

Fender Jeff Beck Strat Signature Model

*Fender Ritchie
Blackmore Strat
Signature Model*

*Fender Buddy Guy
Strat Signature
Model*

Fender Eddie Van
Halen Frankenstein
Limited Run

Fender Stevie Ray Vaughan Strat
Signature Model

Fender Squier P-Bass

Fender Jazz Bass 5-String

Fender Telecaster Road Worn Model

*Gibson Ace Frehley
Budokan with Seymour
Duncan Pearly Gates*

CHAPTER 4

Orville Gibson

It's hard to believe that Gibson guitars trace their roots back to the nineteenth century. Guitars have become so integrated and intertwined with the twentieth-century rock stars; it's astonishing that it all started in the 1890s in the workshop of Orville Gibson. But he created something that no one had before him, the carved archtop for the mandolin and guitars, like the violin. This design made the instruments louder than any of their contemporary fretted instruments, and Orville found himself in high demand. This was very important later with the guitarists in Western swing bands and orchestras. Orville had a very unconventional way of building instruments, which was probably his great key to success; it's always those who think outside of the norm who succeed. He would carve the tops and backs of the instruments, but wouldn't use the conventional method of heating and bending for the sides, rather using wood cut out from solid wood pieces for his sides. Orville's other secret approach was his lack of using internal braces for his archtops. He believed it would deaden the sound, which is why his instruments were louder. Even more impressive was that Orville had no formal training as a luthier or instrument maker. The Gibson company was formed by a group

Gibson Super 400 Model

of businessmen in Kalamazoo, Michigan, in 1902 and called Gibson Mandolin-Guitar Mfg. Co., Ltd. Unfortunately, Orville was pushed out of the company and only received a small royalty until his death in 1918.

In the beginning years of the company Gibson offered an array of fretted instruments, but as demand had it the mandolin was the most popular. The guitar ironically didn't take off until the 1920s with the immortal L-5 designed by Lloyd Loar in 1922. This was a handsomely-crafted instrument with a carved spruce top and was the forefather of the later Super 400.

Even as loud as the L-5 was acoustically it still found itself drowned out by the horns, piano, and drums on stage. So it was a natural move to electrify the guitar in the 1930s, but we got even louder with Marshalls in the '60s! So in 1936 Gibson was the first major manufacturer to release an electric guitar, the ES-150, boasting one single coil pickup, which later became the Charlie Christian guitar. This guitar was sold with an amplifier as a package for $150, consequentially becoming the ES-150. Funny enough it was called the Electric Spanish guitar (ES) because of the popularity of this style of guitar playing

Gibson ES-175 Model

at the time. Even though the guitar was not very clear sounding, was very bass heavy sonically, and prone to wicked feedback, it was a start to keep up with the large orchestras of the day.

Charlie Christian is a very important musical figure in history for more reasons than just being one of the first guitarists to use the electric guitar. He was also a race breaker in the notorious world of white big bands of the time. He became the first black musician who played in the popular big band led by Benny Goodman. By the age of twenty-three, Christian dominated the jazz and swing scene and was voted to the Metronome All-Stars held by *Metronome Magazine.* Ironically, Christian's guitar tone was more similar to a horn than that of a conventional guitar tone. Unfortunately, the brash tone of Goodman and the wailing band noises drowned out many of the guitar nuances, overshadowing much of Christian's recordings. However, the die was cast, and Christian paved the way for such greats as Wes Montgomery, Les Paul, B.B. King, Santana, and Jimi Hendrix.

Gibson Byrdland Florentine

Gibson ES-137 Classic Model

Also in the '30s Gibson developed lap steel guitars that had their origin in the Hawaiian Islands from the nineteenth century. Gibson designed the double neck electric Hawaiian. The two necks could come in any configuration, six, seven, or eight strings. Also the single neck version was the EH-150, which was another of Gibson's electric instruments in 1938. But it wasn't until the '40s that Gibson began making redesigns to the archtop bodies, with a single cutaway. Before that it never occurred to anyone that a guitarist would want to play a high note, mainly because no one would hear it acoustically. But now with more sophisticated pickup electronics those high notes could finally be heard! This is when they started using the pointed cutaway as seen in the ES-175 and later the ES-137.

Gibson 50th Anniversary ES-335 Body

Gibson 50th Anniversary ES-335 Back

Late in the 1950s Gibson launched its double cutaway ES-335, which was the best of both worlds of an archtop and a solid body. It was made up of a solid piece of wood through the middle of the guitar following the neck to the butt, with hollow sides underneath the F holes. This was to reduce feedback that plagued many players with the traditional archtops. It found a loyal home with blues men to jazz fusion cats. Larry Carlton told me that he bought his original ES-335 in a music store in 1969 and it was magic at first touch. All he did was replace the trapeze tailpiece with a hard tailpiece because of tuning issues. However, even with the semihollow body, feedback was still a problem. Players like B.B. King used to stuff newspaper in the F holes to prevent feedback in the ES semihollow bodies. That's why his guitar Lucille is designed with no F holes, which is one of my favorite axes.

If Orville Gibson were alive today he would be astounded at how his legacy and namesake had advanced and become such an incredible guitar-making powerhouse. Especially since he was self-taught and started in a small workshop in Michigan making such unique designs as zithers (originating from Eastern Europe, part of the harp family). Just think, from the zither to the Les Paul then to the Gibson Moderne. Proud heritage!

Gibson Moderne Model

Gibson 50th Anniversary SG 12-String Model

Gibson 1959 Korina Flying V

Gibson ES-339 Model

Gibson Explorer Tremolo Guitar

Gibson Flying V Bass Guitar

Gibson Flying V Tremolo Guitar

Gibson 2000 Explorer

Gibson ES-335 Dot Reissue

Gibson Grabber II Bass

Gibson Firebird Reissue

Gibson SG Angus Young Model

Gibson SG Standard Cherry Model

Gibson Midtown Model

Gibson Midtown Model Body

Zakk Wylde (Ozzy/Black Label Society)
with His Gibson Les Paul Signature Guitar

Gibson 1952 Les Paul Tribute—Body

CHAPTER 5

Les Paul

Les Paul Les Paul
Les Paul Les Paul

Les Paul is responsible for so many inventions it's mind boggling; he was like the Thomas Edison of music. However, one of my favorite stories comes from a good friend of mine and mentor, Geoff Gray, on how he met Les Paul back in the early 1970s.

Before Les Paul's popularity in the '30s he had established a good friendship with Epi Stathopoulo, Epiphone's owner. Because of their relationship, Epi allowed him to work in the Epiphone factory after hours. So Les got started in developing a solid body, first by taking a simple 2 x 4 and mounting pickups, a bridge, and headstock. Les took this idea to Gibson in the early stages, and Gibson basically laughed at the design—just a stick with pickups. The breakthrough really came when Fender launched their Broadcaster, the first official electric guitar. Through various revisions on the design Gibson finally was forced to give in to the new phase of the business, the solid body electric guitar. In 1952 the world saw the very first Gibson Les Paul, and rock 'n' roll was changed forever.

"In 1973 I returned home to find a note from my roommate saying, 'Old man called about your guitar.' I was running an ad in The Want Ad Press, *a New Jersey publication, for a 1956 Gibson J160E with a Les Paul pickup. I placed the return call, and the voice at the other end asked me to describe the instrument. I said it had a P90 Les Paul pickup at the base of the neck. He cut in, 'It's not a P90.' I fired back that it was but that it just didn't have a cover on it. The response was an in-depth rebuttal regarding how it was optimized as an acoustic pickup, etc., etc. I said, 'How do you know all this stuff?' He shot back 'I'm Les Paul.' Without faltering, I said, 'I have so much to learn from you . . . can we ever meet?' Les said, 'What are you doing now, here's where I live.' I said, 'I'm grabbing my car keys as we speak.' One half hour later, that ubiquitous left-hand shake started a journey for me that changed my life for the better.*

This led me to buy my first 4-track Ampex tape machine from Les. That action propelled me into my career, and a thousand more questions followed. Les was much more accessible at that point in his life than in later years when he was 'rediscovered.' I got to be somewhat of an insider, spending many late nights with him, his son Russ, Ralph the maintenance guy, and Wally, Les' sweet brother-in-law. I accompanied Les to many shows: Storyville, Saratoga Performing Arts Center with B.B. King, the MOMA museum gig with George Benson, Bucky Pizzarelli, and Gabor Szabo, college gigs for the filming of The Wizard of Waukesha *and the early Ramada Inn gigs. It was usually just Les and me driving to the gig in the old Chevy, CB radio code name 'the Red Wagon.' Les loved people and was one of the most humorous guys I've ever met. After a late night in his Mahwah kitchen, where Les held court and served popcorn, I would wake up with sore abs as if I'd done 200 sit-ups and then remember how much we'd laughed. An audience of 1 or 3,000 is still an audience. Vaudeville taught Les well.*

Historically before Les, when an audio recording of a performance was made, it was captured live in the studio with no options for overdubs. But Les claimed, 'I'm going back in time to change that note, add a harmony guitar part, and double Mary's vocal.' Everyone said, 'Impossible!' 'Can't be done.' Words that Les ate up and spit out. Even before tape machines, when recordings were made direct to lathe in his garage, Les had the ideal of bouncing from lathe to another and concurrently adding additional parts to the original recording. In 1957 Les delivered a written paper to the Audio Engineering Society suggesting an ideal music device, "Would be something you could carry in your pocket that had no moving parts and held every song you ever wanted to hear." He also invented the Les Paulverizer, the fretted bass, the headless guitar, the solid body electric guitar, and the multitrack tape machine. This CD honors one of the greatest citizens of planet Earth. I'm so glad his contributions were in music. Thank you my dear friend Les for giving me so much in my life and for all you've given to the music world."

—Geoff Gray, Recording Engineer, Far & Away Studios

Gibson 1959 Les Paul "Goldie"

Les Paul and Brian Tarquin at The Iridium (NYC)

I was very fortunate to have known Les and had been honored in visiting his house in Mahwah back in the early '90s with Geoff Gray. I was an assistant engineer at the time and was really taking it all in like a sponge. It was an incredible experience to see Les in his environment and to be in his recording studio. It was like visiting the Gibson and Ampex factory all in one shot. He would be making pickups in his kitchen and hot waxing the pots while eating popcorn and carrying on a conversation without missing a beat, something extraordinary for a then seventy-five-year-old man. I was really taken aback when I learned how he recorded the early Mary Ford and Les Paul Trio albums. He'd record the band during the day in his apartment on a lathe. First you have to understand what a lathe does. It's used in making unique sound grooves on wax cylinders, which are then pressed onto vinyl records. So picture it: Les had a couple of lathe machines in his apartment recording the band on the original disc, then played it back while

recording it on the other lathe along with overdubs of Mary's vocals and his guitar parts. Literally before multitrack recorders, only a man of his tremendous ingenuity could pull it off.

Gibson 50th Anniversary 1960 Les Paul "Black Beauty"

Gibson Les Paul Junior

Gibson Les Paul Junior Body

In 1955 Gibson introduced the Les Paul Junior, which was a scaled-down model with one pickup and the Special with two pickups, bridge, and neck. Both guitars had a flat top instead of the carved tops and were very simply designed.

But the real pinnacle to the Les Paul design was inventor Seth Lover and his PAF (patent applied for) pickup, in short it stopped the P-90 pickups from humming. Much like Fender Strat single coil pickups, the P-90s were prone to getting various

60-cycle hum noises from surrounding lights and other electronic equipment. To avoid the hum, Seth took two coils and wired them out of phase with reverse magnet polarities, so the result was the birth of the humbucker! The DNA of rock 'n' roll was complete now with the Les Paul and the humbucker pickups, tone that would change the rest of the century.

Gibson Jeff Beck Les Paul Model

Gibson Jeff Beck Les Paul Model-Body

Gibson Jimmy Page Les Paul Model

Gibson 1977 Les Paul Deluxe with Seymour Duncan Mini Humbuckers

In 1963, with Les Paul in the middle of a messy divorce from Mary Ford and their waning musical popularity, Gibson stopped making Les Paul guitars. They wouldn't be reintroduced again until 1968 because of high demand from the public. In 1969 Gibson launched the Les Paul Deluxe, my personal favorite with the mini humbuckers, which

Gibson 1959 Mike Bloomfield Les Paul Standard

is the best of both worlds (P-90s and humbuckers). Interestingly enough it took the British Invasion for us Americans to appreciate what we had right here at home, blues and Les Pauls!

*Gibson 1997 Les
Paul Custom with
Seymour Duncan
Humbuckers*

Gibson Les Paul Traditional with Bigsby Bridge

Gibson Lou Pallo Les Paul Signature Model

Gibson Ace Frehley Budokan Les Paul with Seymour Duncan Pickups—Body

*Gibson Ace Frehley Budokan
Les Paul with Seymour Duncan
Pickups*

Gibson Ace Frehley Budokan Les Paul Custom—Back

Gibson Les Paul Custom
Green Flametop Model

Gibson Les Paul Custom Rosewood Maduro Model

Gibson Les Paul
Goldtop Model

Gibson Alex Lifeson Les
Paul Axcess Model

Gibson Randy Rhoads
Les Paul Custom

Gibson Sammy Hagar
Chickenfoot Les Paul

Gibson Les Paul Classic
Custom Model

Gibson 1950s Les Paul Studio Tribute

Stanley Clarke Playing His Alembic Bass

CHAPTER 6

Guitar Designers

*Alembic Cocoa
Model*

Alembic

Alembic has a long history dating back to the golden age of rock music. The company was formed in the Bay Area of California by Ron and Susan Wickersham, who worked closely with such iconic bands as the Grateful Dead, Jefferson Airplane, and Crosby, Stills, Nash & Young. In the early 1970s, it built its first bass guitar for Jack Cassidy of Jefferson Airplane, which for the time was quite exorbitant, priced at over $4,000. It was made of zebrawood that Ron hand carved. An inlay that displayed the "Tree of Life" was inserted on the fingerboard. The pickups were adjustable and were active electronics through a super filtering system. The bass looked like no other on the marketplace, possessing an extremely unique design for the modern world of music. Then in 1972 history was made when Stanley Clarke played his first Alembic bass, which gave the company star power from that point forward. The bass guitar had never had a company so dedicated in making the instrument so fine-tuned and designed.

Alembic Cosmic Glow Model

Alembic Double Duty Model

Alembic Mary's Wish Model

Alembic She Model

Alembic Golden Girl Model

Alembic The Love Giver Model

B.C. Rich 40th Anniversary Bich Model

B. C. Rich

It's hard to believe that a heavy metal guitar company bloomed out of the fine handcrafted flamenco guitar-building of Bernardo "Bernie" Chavez Rico. In 1969, Bernie officially started manufacturing guitars in L.A. at Bernardo's Guitar Shop, building Gibson copies of the Les Paul and the bass EB-3 model, which are very rare to come by today. In 1972, the Seagull design was born with a heel-less neck through body design, which was unique for the time. As the 1970s moved forward so did Bernie's designs, which included the Mockingbird, the Eagle, the Bich, and finally in the 1980s, the Warlock. I remember seeing the Bich when it showed up at Sam Ash on 48th Street in New York City. The shape of the guitar with the natural mahogany finish with those tuning pegs on the body of the guitar was so cool! I know I wanted to pick one up, just for the cool factor itself! These guitars were immediately gravitating to the heavy metal bands of the 1980s with their sharp pointed designs and sexy curves. This was a match made in metal hell! Where would Kerry King of Slayer be without his B.C. Rich Warlock V 7-string or his King V Tribal? The company made a huge effort to connect with bands from the scene, as we see today with their roster of guitarists.

B.C. Rich 40th Anniversary Eagle Model

B.C. Rich 40th Anniversary Mockingbird Model

B.C. Rich 40th Anniversary Seagull Model

B.C. Rich Bich Supreme 8-String Model

B.C. Rich Chuck Schuldiner Tribute Stealth Model

B.C. Rich Draco Supreme Flametop Model

B.C. Rich Draco Supreme Model

B.C. Rich Gunslinger Snakeskin Model

B.C. Rich Gunslinger Model

B.C. Rich Kerry King Signature V Generation 2 Model

B.C. Rich Kerry King Signature V Model—Red

B.C. Rich Mockingbird SL Model

B.C. Rich Stealth Deluxe Model

Carvin Guitars

Many people may not know that Carvin Guitars has been around as long as its longtime rival Fender. A man by the name of Lowell Kiesel opened up the company under the name of the L. C. Kiesel Company and then in 1949 changed the name to Carvin. It started out as a guitar accessory company and then soon branched out to building guitars, basses, and amps. Lowell himself made the early instruments, but he also sold remarked guitars by Harmony and Kay. Later in the 1960s, Carvin used Hofner parts to make many of its own instruments. Then in 1975, Carvin moved its manufacturing facilities to a larger space in Escondido. It was during this time that Carvin started to offer custom options to its customers like Craig Chaquico of Jefferson Starship and Steve Vai. By the end of the 1980s, it made primarily neck through body guitars, as opposed to the Strat-style bolt-on necks. Like many manufacturers today it offers a huge line of artist signature guitars and amplifier series: Steve Vai, Craig Chaquico, Allan Holdsworth, Bunny Brunel, Timothy B. Schmit, and Frank Gambale.

Carvin Allan Holdsworth Signature Model

Carvin Brian Bromberg Signature 4-String Bass Model

Carvin Brian Bromberg Signature 5-String Bass Model

Carvin 4-Bolt Plus C Model

Carvin C66M Model

Carvin C66T Model

Carvin CS4S Model

Carvin CT3M Model

Carvin DC127-12 Model

Carvin DC127M Model

Carvin DC127T Model

Carvin DC400T Model

Carvin ST300M Model

Carvin TL60 Model

Carvin TLB60 Model

Carvin ST300 Model

Charvel

Charvel is synonymous with the L.A. hard rock scene of the late 1970s through the 1980s. In fact, you can trace its DNA to Eddie Van Halen and his two-hand guitar tapping, which changed the guitar forever. Van Halen himself tells the story of going to the Charvel factory in L.A. and picking out cheap second bodies and necks that he could use to make his Frankenstein creation. Man, back then it was a Charvel world! I remember being in an elevator with two other musicians in college, vicariously listening to their conversation. The one guy was a guitarist, and he wanted to join the other guy's band, but the stipulation was that he had to have a Charvel with a Floyd Rose; however, the guitarist said he couldn't afford it! So unfortunately he didn't make the band. I thought, man, what a ridiculous request, but it was a sign of the times—didn't matter how you played, you just had to look the part. Nothing against Charvel, they made a solid hot rod electric guitar with many functions that were custom-oriented for the time. Steve Vai had a nice green one back in the day; in fact, I believe he recorded *Flex-Able* with that beast. And who could forget Jake E. Lee on "Bark at the Moon" with that white Charvel and his band Badlands! Fun times if you can remember it!

Charvel Desolation DST Model

Charvel Desolation DST-3 Model   *Charvel Desolation DX-1 Model*

Charvel Desolation DX-1 Model

Charvel San Dimas Model

Danelectro

Like many manufacturers we've seen who started their roots firmly during World War II, Danelectro was no exception. It was founded in 1947 by Nathan Daniel, an amplifier builder for Epiphone. He started the company making amps for the Sears & Roebuck Company and Montgomery Ward. It wasn't until the mid-1950s that Nathan added guitars to his catalog and subsequently manufactured guitars and amps for the Airline and Silvertone brands. To save on costs and to increase productivity, he eventually changed his materials to plywood and masonite and developed the lipstick pickup design in which the whole electronic mechanism would fit into a silver tube design. These were meant to be simple guitars at an affordable cost. The company was eventually sold to MCA in the mid-1960s, and the new Coral line was introduced, sporting new models of hollow bodies and sitars. However, by the end of the 1960s the party was over, and MCA closed down the company.

Danelectro 12-String Double Cutaway Model

Danelectro 6-String Model

Danelectro Double Cutaway Black Model

Danelectro Double Cutaway Copper Model

Danelectro Double Cutaway White Model

Danelectro Double Cutaway Psychedelic Model

Danelectro Hornet Black Model

Danelectro Hornet Butterscotch Model

Danelectro Hornet Limey Model

Danelectro Longhorn Copperburst Model

Dean Black Candy Model

Dean

It's hard to believe that Dean Zelinsky founded the company back in 1976 when he was only seventeen years old. Like many other guitarists, he pined for a Gibson Flying V, but once he got it, he sawed it right down the middle, so he could see how it was made. Being a true entrepreneur and luthier, he used to take tours of the Gibson plant in Kalamazoo, Michigan, to see what kind of machinery he would need to start up his own guitar company. So off he went, determined to establish his own manufacturing company in Chicago and take the world by storm. In fact, he did take the world by storm, creating those memorable risqué advertisements that featured bikini-clad beauties holding Flying V guitars. Who could forget those ads in *Guitar Player* magazine back in the 1970s, especially if you were a teenager at the time? At the age of twenty-one, Dean achieved rock star notoriety when *People* magazine did a feature on him and his popular guitars. This was quite a departure from other guitar manufacturers that seemed to stay low-key to the outside world. After he reached global domination of his brand by the end of the 1980s, Dean sold the company to Oscar Medeiros, who later in the 1990s sold it to Armadillo Enterprises. But the Dean spirit never left the guitars, and today Dean still serves as an outside consultant and designer.

Dean Bikini Girl

Dean V Anniversary Model

Dean Razorback Union Jack Model

Dean Dime Razorback Model

Dean Rock Your Baby Advertisement

Leslie West with His Dean Signature Model Recording at Jungle Room Studios with Randy Coven

Eastman

Eastman guitars were born out of the passion and dedication of a Chinese immigrant student, Qian Ni, in the 1990s. He originally formed the Eastman Strings company and imported stringed instruments from China, but soon established an in-house workshop that hand made violins. Qian had many master builders craft violins, and in the process they used very few power tools, but instead utilized old-world traditions of woodworking with chisels and scrapers. With the success of the violin, Qian saw the need for affordable archtop guitars and established a workshop to concentrate on guitar building. Incredibly, they built these instruments exactly in the same manner luthiers had in the nineteenth century, which speaks volumes in a world full of so many advance technologies and shortcuts. Master builders of Eastman painstakingly take the time to choose the right selections of tonewoods such as spruce and maple. Every bend and curve is created by hand with no computers, assembly lines, or mass production machines, a true art in itself.

Eastman Jazz Archtop

Eastwood Guitars

Have you ever wondered what happened to those strange and futuristic guitars that used to sell in the Montgomery Ward catalogs back in 1960s? Well look no further, because guitar enthusiast Mike Robinson of Eastwood Guitars has unearthed them! He has taken the Airline series guitars and replicated them in the Far East to achieve affordability and accuracy. They were originally built by the Valco manufacturing company for Montgomery Ward's mail order catalog and have now become in vogue with the new generation of guitarists like Jack White of the White Stripes. The real difference between the Eastwood models and the originals from the long-ago defunct Valco Company is that the original bodies were made of "Res-O-Glas" while the replica bodies by Eastwood are made of chambered mahogany wood. Now because of the new popularity of the vintage Airline series, prices have jumped through the roof the past few years, which makes the Eastwood models a smart choice for the new generation of guitarists. Mike is busy adding three to four models per year to his stock, including Wandre Tri-Lam, Breadwinner, Airline Tuxedo Custom, Messenger, Supro Dual Tone, Airline Bighorn, Doral, P-90 Special, and the Classic 12.

Eastwood Classic 12-String Guitar

Eastwood Airline 1959 2-Pickup

Eastwood Airline 1959 Coronado

Eastwood Airline H44 Deluxe

Eastwood Airline Tuxedo Deluxe

Eastwood Airline Tuxedo Custom

Eastwood GP Model

Eastwood Hi-Flyer Phase 4

Eastwood Airline Folkstar

Eastwood Airline Coronado Standard

Eastwood Airline Lap Steel

Eastwood Airline Map Bass

Eastwood Airline Map Model

Eastwood Breadwinner Model

Eastwood Classic 4 Bass

Ed Roman

Before Ed Roman was a guitar builder he sold pro audio gear back in the '70s to such prominent people as Eddie Kramer, Phil Spector, John Lennon, Alan Parsons, Willie Nelson, Ed Germano, Tony Bongiovi, and Phil Ramone. The store, East Coast Sound, was located in Connecticut 60 miles from New York just over the state line, and the prices were 20 percent lower than the New York pro audio dealers. However, by the mid-'90s the pro audio business was being killed by the home-studio business, making it the perfect storm. The combination of affordability and technology really put the kibosh on high-end pro audio dealers. So in 1995, Ed concentrated on making guitars and produced numerous brands of boutique guitars: Abstract, Baker, Centurion, J Frog, LSR, Pearlcaster, Lowrider, Scorpion, Schon, Mosrite, JET, Quicksilver. The following is an interview with Scott Krell from Ed Roman Guitars.

Ed Roman Abstract Rockingbird Guitar

Ed Roman Black Korina 2000

Can you give us a little background on your-self and how you got started with guitar building and why you started making custom guitars?

After working years in traditional independent music stores and working as a musician, I was contacted by Ed Roman in early 2002 when he was bringing his operation to Las Vegas. Ed Roman was already very well known in the industry, and I liked the fact that besides selling traditional branded guitars, he had a unique insight into building, modifying, and creating guitars that were in some cases something that would separate the player from the crowd. Being a working musician and working on my own instruments I always appreciated new ideas and new ways to catch the attention of an audience. There was always something on my own guitars that I felt would make them more to my personal tastes, so the idea of working with a manufacturer as well as a retailer seemed like an excellent match. In a very theatrical way, he made me an offer that I could not refuse, and I started working with him upon his arrival in Las Vegas immediately.

It seems that in the world of CNC manufacturing, the art of the guitar luthier is lost. How did you come up with the unique designs and what makes your guitars so different?

Ed had explained his take on getting into building to me as well. It was certainly born out of the love of certain types of guitars, but being of an independent mind he always would catch the shortcomings, which he often blamed on business models that shortchange quality for quantity. He also felt the word "custom" was thrown around as a model name or a short list of choices, when it should have

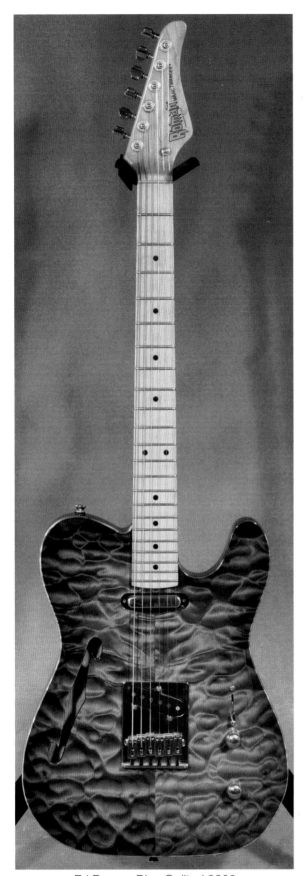

Ed Roman Blue Quilted 2000

a much more unlimited meaning. Just because a guitar model name is custom doesn't actually make it a custom guitar for the eventual player of that instrument. I have always respected that philosophy and sense of individuality, which is getting hard to find in today's world.

What is the most challenging thing about making your guitars?

In a mass production world it is always a challenge to "redesign the wheel," and this is a challenge shared on the custom side as well, as making unique truly custom instruments have careful checks and balances. It can look wild or tame, but it does have to play well, feel good, and sound great. Often it starts with a body design, but really that is one of the more cosmetic aspects in guitar building and design, particularly with solid bodied electric guitars. Yet, that is the first thing people notice, so coming up with unique designs is always a topic of discussion. Many are derived from obvious inspirations, but one can also look to many other types of instruments or things in general for this inspiration as well. Implementing the design into a functional instrument is of the greatest importance. The type of build is extremely important to the overall quality as well. We employ several build designs and techniques because they each have their own reflection on the eventual tonality of the finalized instrument. Build designs like neck through, three-quarter deep set neck tenon, set neck, glued or bolted (often referred to as bolt in) as well as bolt on—all have a serious impact on the overall sound of the instrument. Ed Roman often said the heart of the guitar is how the neck attaches to the body, and I have always agreed with that.

But wait, there's more!

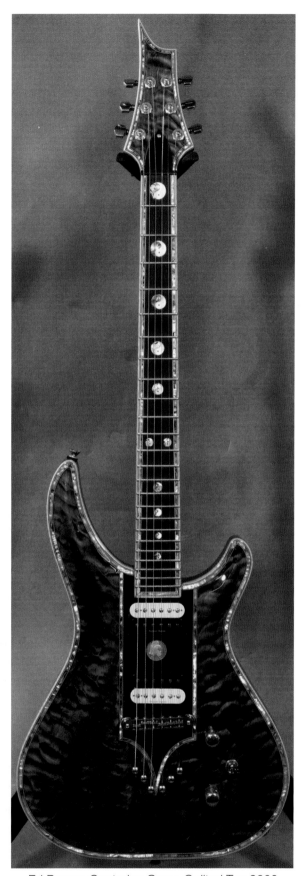

Ed Roman Centurion Green Quilted Top 2000

There are many choices out there beyond the build look or design of the guitar, the hardware, pickups, electronics, and so on. At Ed Roman guitars we also offer insights into how that is done. The philosophy of "Direct Tonal Transfer" is something that we also hold of great importance. It really is simple physics in that getting from point A to B should have the least resistance, the least loss of vibration, tone, and sound. We utilize several techniques to achieve this and direct coupling is one of the most popular ways of achieving this. People are very familiar with "Direct Mounting" of the pickups to the body, but on our premier line of guitars, the Quicksilver, for example we have taken that a step further by directly coupling the neck through the pickup to the body. By utilizing a tenon that extends past the neck pickup we are able to achieve that. More importantly, we have found this will deliver a cleaner neck pickup without the loss of bass response and will reduce the lower midrange murkiness that can be found in some instruments. The final step of this example is utilizing inserts into the body, so the screws can be tightened to a great degree without fearing any wood damage that some traditional guitars might suffer. Again, we have found a tonal clarity by utilizing this particular technique.

Can you take us through your process of building from choosing the right wood to the paint finishing?

There is always a challenge in every custom guitar build and usually one of the popular things brought up by a client is the wood choice. People want pretty woods that reflect their personal character, but also tonally sound woods and combinations of woods that help define their sound. Once again there are many choices. Choosing the right woods

Ed Roman Quilted Top Double Cutaway

is important on several levels. Not just with respect to looks and sound, but one must consider how it will hold up as well and from a builder's standpoint: how difficult is it to work with? The last one being important to the people working with it, thereby translating into the cost, which is important to the builder when a price is quoted. Fortunately, there are many good choices out there. When building a custom guitar for someone we must take all their personal preferences, sonic and visual, and come up with the right combination of choices. This can be very easy when using the popular standards, but can be a bit more challenging when someone wants to get something completely different from that. Learning by experience (the hard way) is how many of us have learned things. I would also suggest reading on the tonal properties of woods with respect to the desired instrument.

There always seems to be a debate about the finishes—nitro vs. poly. What is the difference and how does it affect the tone of the instrument?

The finishing of the guitar is an interesting thing and has been often the topic of many debates. An oiled finish tends to allow more resonance, allowing the wood to "breathe" somewhat, where gloss finishes tend to encase the guitar body in what is essentially a tomb of glue, but it is shiny and offers a complementary cosmetic appeal for many. Gloss finishes are more durable as well, but a well-cared-for oiled finish can be easy to maintain as well. Then there is the great debate of polys and nitro. One of the advantages that many talk about with a nitro finish is that it seeps into the wood over time, allowing the wood to resonate more, hence the "mellowing with age" term often used for vintage guitars. If you have twenty years, give

Ed Roman Flatbat Model

or take, and don't mind the yellowing discoloration (many prefer that aging as well), then that may be for you. The poly finishes tend to be more durable, and stay much more clear, but are less likely to mellow. One must also take into account the thickness of the finish, which can add or detract in the overall tone of the guitar. The whole finish argument is even more important in acoustic instruments, and I don't think it will ever be a finished debate—that is why we happily offer a customer choice as to which type of finish would best suit them.

Do you wind your own pickups or use a third party and how important are the electronics in your guitars?

The electronics: Although we at Ed Roman Guitars do not wind our own pickups, we do offer a variety of well-made pickups, and I must say that the electronics are of great importance to any electric guitar. This is a bit more challenging because of the subjective flavor of what a person wants to hear. You can do everything else perfectly to a client's liking, but the wrong type of pickups can be a setback. I say setback because fortunately, pickups are easily removable and there are many to choose from. Knowing the customer's preference for music, what they like to play, who do they like the tone of, are all important questions to ask. Luckily, there are a great many high-quality pickups out there that can offer a nice variety of choices for various tastes. I mentioned earlier about the direct mounting of the pickups as well, which is an excellent option to choose for clarity, tonality, and sustain.

ESP

During the 1970s, a Tokyo company emerged by the name of Electric Sound Products (ESP) that supplied aftermarket replacement parts for guitars. But it wasn't until the mid-1980s when it made its way to New York City and opened a store, first on 19th Street and then on 48th Street, that it made its mark on U.S. soil. It also made custom guitars there for Kiss guitarist Vinnie Vincent and Ron Wood of The Rolling Stones. I remember the store on 48th Street well; I used to go down and buy blank necks when I was building guitars in the '80s. It was a fantastic store, and it was a great loss to the NYC guitar community when it closed. It had all sorts of prefinished bodies with outrageous graphics and a cornucopia of guitar parts and accessories. During this same time it became the OEM supplier to such popular guitar companies as Kramer, Robin, and Schecter. But then as fate would have it, Dokken guitar shredder George Lynch visited the ESP store in Japan and the Kamikaze model was born. Again, like other manufacturers of the time it aligned itself with the top guitarists like James Hetfield and Kirk Hammett of Metallica plus Dave Mustaine from Megadeth. In the '90s, the company came out with the LTD brand, which were made in Korea and composed of lower end components, which made them more affordable to the consumer. Hence, they became extremely popular among thrash metal guitarists and metal heads around the world.

ESP Ltd F-414 Bass

ESP Ltd George Lynch Strat

ESP Ltd Les Paul Deluxe

ESP Ltd George Lynch Tiger Stripe Strat

Fernandes Chameleon Purple V

Fernandes

Fernandes Guitars originally started out by building flamenco guitars, but soon became a part of the Japanese guitar invasion in the 1970s. Like many Asian companies, it made a name for itself by making copies of American guitars like the Strat and the Les Paul; it owned the Burny name for its Gibson replicas. At the time, the Fender replicas were considered superior to Fenders themselves because of the poor quality control CBS had in manufacturing Fender Instruments. In fact, Fernandes made these replicas so accurate, right down to the smallest detail, it was eventually sued by both Fender and Gibson and forced to change the headstocks along with other elements. By the 1980s, Fernandes became one of the largest manufacturers in Japan going on to conquer the rest of the world in the 1990s. One of its most popular products was the Fernandes Sustainer, Hendrix feedback in a box! The three basic modes: harmonic mode where the note pitch rises to the fifth natural harmonic, natural mode where the note will continue to ring its natural tone, and finally the mix mode, which blends the natural and harmonic modes to harmonize indefinitely to form harmonized feedback. The sustainer is installed in the Elite and Pro Series guitars or you can buy a kit to install on your own guitar.

Fernandes Dragonfly Elite Amber Double Cutaway

Fernandes Vortex Pro Tobacco Sunburst V

Fernandes Dragonfly Pro Sunburst Double Cutaway

Fernandes Gravity 5-String Bass

Fernandes Monterey 4-String Bass

Fernandes Retrorocket X Lava Flame Strat

Fernandes Revolver X Reverse Headstock Strat

Gander Guitars

Out of the Canadian prairies near Winnipeg, guitar luthier Ray Gander was born. He is the brainchild behind the unusual shapes and exotic woods used in Gander Guitars. One look at his guitars and you will see the detail and time that was put into each design. Again, you can feel and see how each curve and shape has been handcrafted with extreme precision. The Gander flagship guitar, Libra, is made of bloodwood and alder and boosts a fretboard made of ebony inlaid with abalone and bloodwood. Founder Ray Gander explains his expertise on guitar building.

Gander Gemini

Gander Gemini—Headstock

Gander Gemini—Body

Gander Gemini Raw—Body

Gander Gemini Raw—Side View

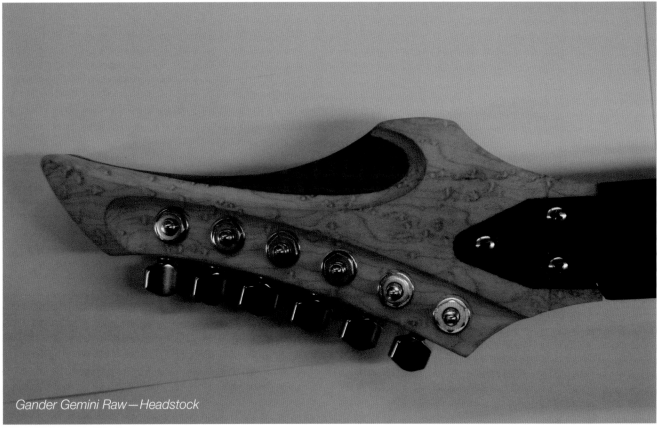

Gander Gemini Raw—Headstock

Can you give us a little background on your-self and how you got started with guitar building and making custom guitars?

I grew up in a very small country town of about three hundred people . . . with no music stores etc. When I reached fifteen and decided I was going to be the next Johnny Cash, I decided to try building my own guitar. The Johnny Cash bit didn't work out as planned, but I did have fun building the guitar. I designed the shape of it because I had never seen a Fender or Gibson up close . . . besides, why build what has already been done? When I was still in my teens, I built a custom show bike from a 650 Yamaha, a unique design hydroplane, and a 1929 Plymouth coupe with a Chrysler hemi motor. I designed all of them based on what I saw in magazines but really had no training other than self-taught. Of all of them . . . the guitar turned out the best and was interesting enough to try building another . . . and another. The bike turned out pretty well too, and I still work on the three motorcycles I currently own.

It seems that in the world of CNC manufacturing, the art of the guitar luthier is lost. How did you come up with the unique designs and what makes your guitars so different?

I have nothing against CNC machines, but I think one that would produce the type of detail that I put into my guitars would either not exist or would be totally cost-prohibitive. Actually, the most enjoyable part of building my guitars is the hand carving of the body shapes . . . I start with a two-dimensional full size drawing, which I trace onto the wood, and from there I don't know how it's going to turn out until I start to carve . . . even the second or third guitar of the same design usually ends up having slight differences, because I want to try some thing a "little different." As far as the designs go . . . I have spent over thirty

years in the design/printing/sign business and have always been "artistic." My schoolbooks had more "doodles" in the margins than work on the pages. I once drew a well-endowed "cowgirl" on the top of my desk during a less than interesting math class and instead of getting in trouble over it, the teachers called each other in to see it, and it stayed there 'till the end of the year. My actual inspiration for my designs of most things was a Porsche 928 that I once saw . . . absolutely every line on that car had a "reason to be there," and as far as I was concerned, every part of the design flowed into the next part . . . that is what I try to achieve with my guitars.

What is the most challenging thing about making guitars?

As I said before, the thing I enjoy most is the biggest part of the guitar . . . carving the body. I guess the most challenging thing about making them is getting the wood ready to carve. The reason for that is that my guitars have a carbon beam inside where it is not seen, that goes from the tuners to the bridge. All the wood that makes up the guitar is assembled and epoxied "around the carbon beam." My unique designs also means that the wood is often made up of several pieces that eventually have to be in exactly the right place to create the finished effect that I was after.

Can you take us through your process of building, from choosing the right wood to the paint finishing?

Certainly the first step toward building one of my guitars is the first doodle that I make of a new design. If I like the look of it I will work on final-izing the doodle until I think it has potential as a final design. I then blow it up to full size and work on the drawing to make sure all the "import-ant bits," such as pickups and the bridge, will fit exactly as they should. If the design has a feature that is determined by the look of the wood, I will choose the wood that I feel will best do the job. Here is where I will likely be chastised by the rest of the luthiers in the world . . . but I believe that if you use good electronics and hardware you can bolt them on a two-by-four and make it sound good . . . of course a Sitka spruce two-by-four would likely help. Because of the strength of the carbon beam, I could choose balsa wood for my neck if I desired, so knowing what woods are at least acceptable as tonewoods . . . I can choose my woods for beauty and grain etc. I use only handheld tools, but let's not get carried away here . . . I'm not talking about a hammer and chisel . . . I think that like "Tim 'the Toolman' Taylor" I own every handheld power tool known to man. I use an angle-driver with a 24-grit sanding disk to rough shape the body . . . sort of like the guy carving the totem pole with a chain saw. I cut out the pickup cavities with a good router, and I do most of the rest of the shaping with an air-driven die-grinder . . . sort of like a Dremel tool on steroids. That still only brings me to the point where I have to start doing the hours and hours of final sanding. The other major part and the most important part of any guitar is a properly made fretboard. I also use only stainless steel frets unless requested otherwise. When all is ready for painting I do my own painting using clear two-part urethane paint tinted with House of Kolor concentrate. Any color is possible, and the paint remains transparent to show the wood underneath. It usually takes a few hand-rubbed coats to do the proper job. I then install the hardware and electronics and the guitar is complete.

There seems to be a debate about nitro vs. poly finishes. What do you think is the difference and how does it affect the tone of the instrument?

As I said, I use two-part automotive urethane on my guitars, and I have great success with it. I use it because I want a finish that is not affected by heat or sweat or anything else the local rock star can throw at it. If it will last outside in the sun, rain, and snow . . . it will surely last on a guitar. Again at the risk of being chastised by fellow luthiers, I don't believe the finish of a guitar measurably affects the tone . . . especially when you realize that some pretty decent guitars are made entirely of plastic, carbon fiber, metal, etc. I shouldn't even comment on lacquers, but a hot rod owner friend of mine had to repaint his entire show car because of the way the lacquer "spider-webbed" from a minor collision.

Do you wind your own pickups or use a third party and how important are the electronics in your guitars?

This brings me to an item that is sort of embarrassing . . . electronics and I don't really get along well. I install all my own pickups, hardware, and electronics by following my book on wiring diagrams etc., but if, after I'm done, it doesn't work the way it's supposed to, I take it to a place in Winnipeg called Ultimate Guitar Works and let the experts take care of it for me. To date, I have only used Seymour Duncan and DiMarzio pickups and top-of-the-line tuners, etc., because as I have said, I believe good electronics are 99 percent of any electric guitar . . . the wood and the "look" of the guitar are there to make the player feel proud to be playing it. I will never get into winding my own pickups but I have thought about working with someone . . . but there is so much quality product already available . . . how do you compete with the likes of Seymour Duncan or any of the other brilliant manufacturers out there?

Godin

As we've seen with other guitar manufacturers, Robert Godin got his start building necks and bodies for other larger guitar companies, before he opened his own factory. As a Canadian guitar designer, he wanted to make his own mark in the guitar world. He created several different brands to appeal to his customers' playing ability, from Norman catering to entry- to mid-level acoustic guitarists and Art & Lutherie making entry-level guitars. The Godin brand itself is delegated to the midrange to high-end marketplace, which uses North American tonal woods. They found a niche market for their synth pickups installed in their top models and using piezo pickups in their bridges on their acoustic guitars. It's nice to see that a guitar manufacturer still considers premium woods when constructing models. Godin gives you a choice of maple or Indian rosewood fingerboard for their models Passion, Velocity, Radiator, SD, Exit 22, and Freeway, and uses premium-grade rock maple in the models Velocity, Redline, Detour, Radiator, SD, Exit 22, Freeway, Classic, and Freeway 4 and 5. They even make an affordable archtop called the 5th Avenue, sporting a beautiful Canadian Wild Cherry body featuring a molded arched top and back, F holes, and the classic tone of a P-90 neck pickup, designed by Godin himself.

Gretsch

This is a company that has a long history in instrument-making dating back to the nineteenth century. The company found its birth from the hands of Friedrich Gretsch, a German immigrant instrument maker, who opened his shop in Brooklyn, New York. Like many of his generation from Europe, he worked hard and strived for quality, not quantity. Starting out as a respected builder of drums and banjos, the early twentieth century saw Gretsch come into its own with archtop guitars. One of its famous models was the Synchromatic line, which was oversized and adorned with ornate designs. By the 1950s, it increased production and developed new less ornate guitars that became very popular, such as the Electromatic, Electro II, and the Synchromatic. By 1955, the hallmark Gretsch

designs came into their own. Models like the Corvette, Country Club, and the Chet Atkins came in brilliant colors like green, red, orange, burgundy, yellow, and white. It also improved features like adjustable saddle bridges, decorative fingerboard inlays, double coil "Filter Tron" pickups, and stereo wiring options on some models. One of the most popular was the White Falcon flashing a 17-inch body, 24-karat gold plating, two DeArmond pickups, and a "Cadillac G" tailpiece with a V-shaped crossbar. Not until 1964, when George Harrison appeared with The Beatles on the *Ed Sullivan Show* playing a Gretsch Country Gentleman, did the company's success soar through roof!

Godin 5th Avenue Jazz Model

Gretsch Chet Atkins Model

Gretsch G5105 Electromatic 3-Pickup Model

Gretsch Lap Steel

Gretsch G6128T-GH George Harrison Signature Duo
Jet Model

Hagström

Hagström roots go back to the 1920s, when a man by the name of Albin Hagström imported accordions from other parts of Europe into Sweden. But it wasn't until 1958 that it started manufacturing guitars. So as you can imagine the early guitars were painted very similar to the accordions with pronounced sparkle and pearloid celluloid finish. Hagström was one of the first manufacturers to attempt to build guitars outside of the United States. It manufactured both solid and hollow bodies, with the later designs named the Jimmy and the Viking, aptly so for a country known for Leif Erikson. In 1961, it also launched bass guitars to the public, including the legendary 8-string bass and the Hagström flagship models Swede and Super Swede. By the early '80s, Hagström had closed its doors, but because of the cult following it had incurred through the years, the twenty-first century has seen Hagström guitars back in production.

Hagström the Viking Model

Hagström Tremar Swede Model

Hagström Northern Swede Model

Hagström Super Swede Model

Hagström Deuce-F Double Cutaway

Hagström Ultra Swede Model

Hagström Viking Bass Model

Hagström XL-5 Strat Model

Hagström HJ 600 Jazz Model

Hamer

Paul Hamer, Jol Dantzig, and John Montgomery founded Hamer Guitars as a boutique custom shop in 1973 for professional guitar players. They were one of the first builders to do so and based many early designs on Gibson's Flying V and Explorer models. Hamer specialized in building guitars for such bands as Kiss, Cheap Trick, Bad Company, and Jethro Tull. But when Frank Untermyer joined the company as partner, Hamer attempted to grow larger in their sales. The '80s saw a lot of new models like the Blitz, Cruisebass, Prototype, Special, and Phantom. They always prided themselves in custom hand-built guitars with hand-chiseled dovetail neck joints to allow a tight final fit so all sides of the joint will transmit vibration. They go through a rigorous slow-drying process on their various woods (maple, mahogany, and rosewood), which reduces breakdown of the wood fiber. Then the wood has to go through months of drying time for an end result of superior resonance and durability. They go through the same detail in their paint finishes, which, as I always remembered, looked like glass when displayed in stores.

Hamer Sunburst Gold Double Cutaway With P-90s

Hamer Californian Quilt Top Strat

Hamer Vector Flametop V

Höfner

Can you say, The Beatles? Well, this is the guitar maker of the famous violin-shaped bass that Paul McCartney played in the early days of The Beatles, appearing on the *Ed Sullivan Show* and at Shea Stadium. Karl Höfner founded the company back in the nineteenth century in Germany and became one of the largest suppliers of stringed instruments. Like Hagström in Sweden, Höfner would serve to give post-WWII European guitarists affordable instruments to play; in the '50s and '60s, American guitars were very pricey in Europe and were hard to find. So the Brits, who were preparing to invade the states, had an alternative to Gibson and Fender guitars, in which Höfner was more than happy to fulfill their needs. Höfner made copies of popular American archtop guitars at the time and called them the Club 40 and Club 50. It also made Fender-like solid bodies, calling them the 175 and the Galaxie. But the die had been cast when Paul McCartney and The Beatles

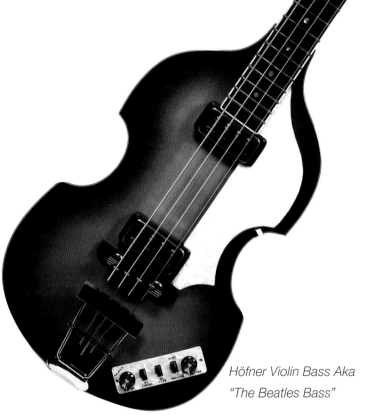

Höfner Violin Bass Aka "The Beatles Bass"

were on tour in Germany and he switched to bass in Hamburg. The world would always remember Höfner for that quirky-looking violin Beatles bass.

Ibanez

The company has a long history and over fifty years of innovation under its belt, becoming a prominent guitar manufacturer. Its name was cleverly taken from a nineteenth-century classical guitar builder in Spain, Salvador Ibáñez. In Japan, Matsujiro Hoshino started the guitar business early in the twentieth century, eventually forming the Hoshino Musical Instrument Store. But it wasn't until after WWII and the economic recovery of Japan that Hoshino started producing electric guitars for the rock 'n' roll generation of the '50s and '60s, mainly in Japan and Europe. By the early '70s, Ibanez was making several copies of Gibson Les Pauls, SGs, Flying

Vs, Explorers, Epiphone hollow bodies, and even Fenders. Because of threatening litigations from Gibson attorneys, Ibanez was forced to stop producing direct copies by the end of the '70s. But who could forget that awesome red candy-striped Ibanez Explorer that Van Halen cut up and played on *Women and Children First,* which changed my world! Even though the Gibson lawsuit derailed Ibanez temporarily, it got back on its feet and produced the artist models of George Benson and Paul Stanley's Iceman. But it wasn't till the '80s that Ibanez came into its own when it endorsed such guitar aficionados as Steve Vai and Joe Satriani, who influenced a generation.

Joe Satriani with His Ibanez Signature Model

*Ibanez Joe Satriani JS20S
20th Anniversary Silver
Surfer Guitar—Body*

*Ibanez Joe Satriani JS20S
20th Anniversary Silver
Surfer Guitar—Close Up*

*Ibanez Joe Satriani JS20S 20th
Anniversary Silver Surfer Guitar*

*Ibanez 8-String with Seymour
Duncan Blackout Pickups*

Ibanez AM93 Hollow Body Model

Ibanez Artcore Custom Model

1980 Ibanez Artist with Seymour Duncan Pickups

Ibanez Jet King Bass

Ibanez Prestige Strat Model

Ibanez RG Series 6-String Strat

Ibanez S 25th Limited Edition Strat

Ibanez Soundgear 4-String Bass

Jackson

The Jackson guitar story is intertwined with its founder Wayne Charvel in San Dimas, California. Grover Jackson was an employee of Wayne's in the '70s and eventually bought the company from him in 1978. The important thing was he made what was later to become the Super Strat, which was very popular since Van Halen's debut album in 1978. Eddie Van Halen created and pioneered the spirit of making the beefed-up atomic guitar. Before Van Halen, no guitar manufacturers offered a Strat-style guitar with a double humbucker in the bridge position and a locking tremolo system. Another big break for Jackson was designing the Flying V for Ozzy guitarist Randy Rhoads in the early '80s. This helped catapult Jackson to popularity among players such as Jeff Beck, Steve Vai, and Vivian Campbell, as well as the jetsetters on the Sunset Strip. Jackson guitars also boasted the jumbo frets and had 24 frets so players could reach those painful high notes!

Jackson Kelly Model

Jackson King V Model

Jackson Soloist Model

Jackson Flying V Randy Rhoads Model

Jay Turser

Similar to the early Ibanez story, Jay Turser is a company that supplies players from entry level to mid-level at a very affordable price. In fact, *Guitar Player* magazine awarded the company Editor's Pick for the JT-LT-RW models in 2011. Its parent company is U.S. Music Corporation in Illinois, and, like many other corporations, it outsources the manufacturing to China. However, it uses real tonewoods such as mahogany, maple, and rosewood for its bodies and necks. As with Ibanez forty years earlier, it bases its designs on tried-and-true American guitars, such as the Les Paul, SG, Strats, and Teles.

Jay Turser SG JT-50 Model

Jay Turser Les Paul JT-220 Model

Jay Turser Les Paul JT-220D Model

Jay Turser SG JT-50 Model—Close-Up

Jay Turser Les Paul JT-220D Model—Serpent Neck Inlay

Jay Turser JT-134 Semihollow Body Model—Close-Up

Jay Turser JT-133 Semihollow Body Model

Jay Turser JT-139 Hollow Body Model

Jay Turser JT-140 Hollow Body Model with Tremolo

Jay Turser JT-200 Pro
Double Cutaway Model

Jay Turser JT-200 Les Paul Model

Jay Turser JT-300 Strat Model

Jay Turser JT-Cleopatra Hollow Body Model

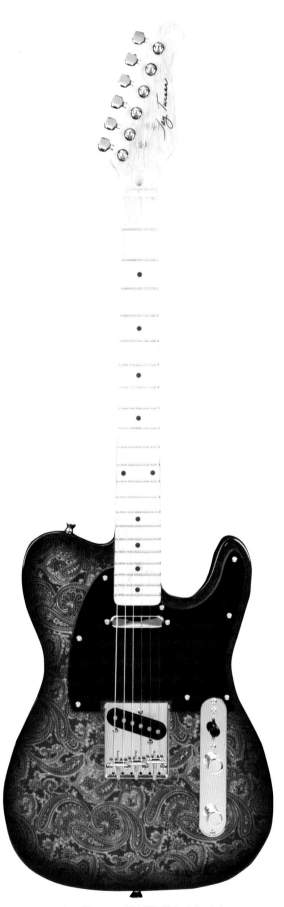

Jay Turser JT-LTP Tele Model

Jay Turser JT-RES Electric Resonator Guitar

Jay Turser JT-XG2 SG Double Neck Model

Jay Turser JTB-402 Precision Bass Model

Jay Turser JT-B2B Violin Bass Model

Kramer

The story of Kramer starts with founder Gary Kramer and his partnership with Travis Bean, a collaboration that created their aluminum guitar design. Crazy design and even crazier to keep in tune. However, Gary moved on and formed his company in 1976 and created his own take on the aluminum guitar, which had a most distinctive headstock—it was split in half. But it wasn't until the birth of the Super Strat in the early '80s that Kramer became a huge manufacturer. All it took was an endorsement from guitar icon Eddie Van Halen, the Floyd Rose Tremolo system, and red candy-striped paint. Voilà! A star is born! Who could forget that banana headstock on their Baretta models? Well, as they say, "Build a field and they shall come," and they did, in droves. Endorsements came from Vivian Campbell, Neal Schon, Elliot Easton, and Richie Sambora.

1983 Kramer Striker Strat with
Seymour Duncan Pickups—Body

The One and Only Eddie Van Halen Tearing It Up with His Kramer Candy Cane Striped 5150 Strat

Kramer Eddie Van
Halen Candy Cane
Striped Signature
Strat—Body

*1984 Kramer Baretta Strat Reissue
with Floyd Rose Tremolo*

Kramer Assault Plus Les Paul Style

*Kramer Assault Les Paul Style
with Floyd Rose Tremolo*

Kramer Assault 220 Model

Kramer Baretta Special Model

Kramer Disciple 4-String Bass

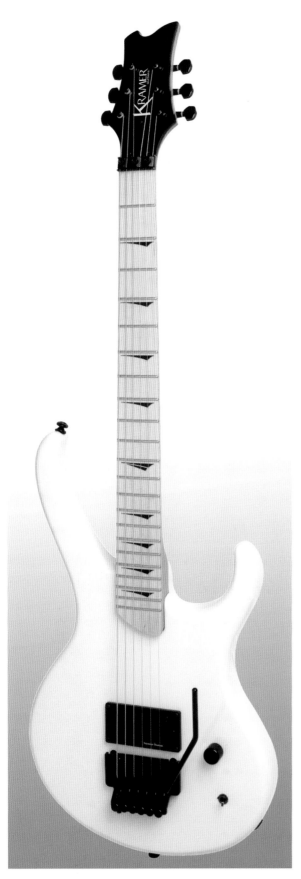

Kramer Disciple 6-String Guitar
With Floyd Rose Tremolo

Kramer Doublecut Guitar

Kramer Nite V Model

*Kramer Nite V Model With
Reverse Headstock*

Kramer Pacer Tiger Striped Strat

Kramer Classic Pacer Model

Kramer Pariah Model

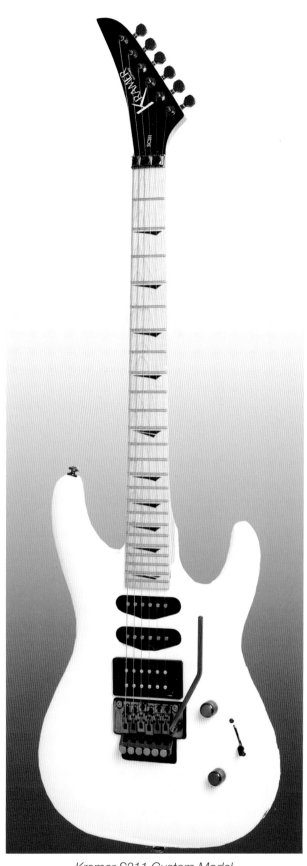

Kramer S211 Custom Model
with Reverse Headstock

Kramer SM-1 Model with Shark Tooth Neck Inlays

Kramer Striker 211 Custom Model

Kramer Striker Bass Model

Kramer Striker 211 Model

Kramer Vanguard Flying V Model

Guitar Legend Steve Morse Playing His Music Man Signature Guitar

Music Man

After Leo Fender sold his company to CBS in 1965, discontentment started between longtime workers and new management. By the early '70s, Leo partnered with two ex-Fender employees, Forrest White and Tom Walker, to form Music Man. They started to make amplifiers and by the mid-'70s moved on to making guitars when Leo's noncompetitive clause was up with CBS. The Stingray and Sabre were the first models added to the lineup. However, by 1980 because of partnership issues, Leo left and formed G&L, and in 1984 Ernie Ball bought Music Man. The Stingray basses were more popular than the Music Man 6-string counterparts. So Ernie Ball made an aggressive effort to get famous guitarist endorsements from Steve Morse, Ron Wood, Keith Richards, and of course Eddie Van Halen. Eddie's signature series was a very popular guitar in the early 1990s, along with the Steve Morse model, the Silhouette.

Music Man John Petrucci
Signature Guitar—Body

Music Man John Petrucci Signature Guitar

Music Man Stingray 4-String Bass

Parker

Ken Parker and electronic-guru partner Larry Fishman set out to buck the system and approach guitar building in a completely different manner than traditional methods. Korg, ironically a keyboard manufacturer, heavily financed the business. These new Fly guitars had piezo pickups, usually used in acoustic guitars, along with traditional magnetic pickups. Parker's theory was the wood was not as essential for tone in electric guitars as it was in acoustic ones. So he used composite materials on the exterior of the wood frame. This enabled the design to be very thin and light, without losing sustain. He also used an unusual flat spring in his whammy bar assembly as well. All in all, the guitar is a true hybrid and attracts players from all styles.

Parker Nitefly Radial Neck Joint Series

Parker Fly Deluxe

Parker Maxxfly Bass

Parker Nitefly Radial Neck Joint with Quilted Top

Parker PDF-60B Model

Parker DF-524N Model

Parker Fly Select Model

Parker Nitefly Radial Neck Joint Model—Close-Up

Parker Fly Deluxe Model—Body

Parker Max Fly Bass—Headstock

PRS

Paul Reed Smith always had a knack of getting through to rock stars and making them custom guitars from the 1970s to the present. Before he was a mass manufacturer, he was building guitars for Ted Nugent, Carlos Santana, and Peter Frampton. By the mid-'80s, Paul raised enough money to open up the doors to his new guitar manufacturing company, PRS. The striking visuals of his guitars were shiny beautiful wood grains with tops from exotic tonewood. He was always known for his double cut- away solid body guitars in the Les Paul style. But once PRS started producing the single cutaway, Gibson was on them like white on rice. Similar to Ibanez, a lawsuit incurred and PRS was forced to drop the man- ufacturing of single cutaways. But you have to hand it to PRS for the lavish price of their guitars; it is one of the few who can hang with the big-boy manufacturers.

Paul Reed Smith 245 Single Cutaway Model

Paul Reed Smith 1957/2008 Custom 24 Model

Jazz Guitarist Denny Jiosa Jamming on His Paul Reed Smith

Rickenbacker

Started by the Swiss immigrant Adolf Rickenbacher, Rickenbacker has a long, illustrious heritage. Like contemporaries of the time, they produced the electric Spanish guitar and lap steels. But as with Fender and Gibson, the gold rush didn't come until the British Invasion. So much so that many people thought Rickenbacker was a British manufacturer judging from the number of English bands playing their instruments: The Beatles, The Who, The Rolling Stones. Just one listen to "A Hard Day's Night" and you knew it was a Rickenbacker with the jangly tonal characteristics. You can even hear it with American artists like Roger McGuinn from The Byrds and his distinctive Rickenbacker 12-string tone on "Eight Miles High." Once again, it took the British Invasion for us Americans to appreciate our own homegrown instruments.

Rickenbacker 660 12-String Model

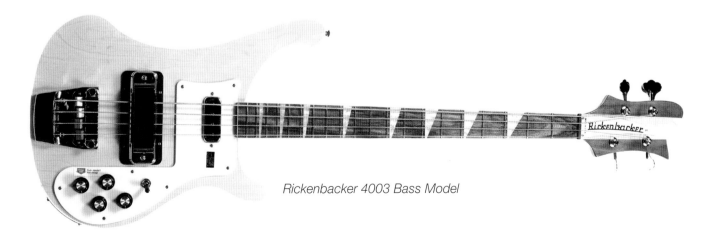

Rickenbacker 4003 Bass Model

Roland VG Guitar Headstock

Roland

This is a company not known for guitar manufacturing, but for the synth innovations of the twentieth century and how it applied them to the guitar. In the 1970s, it launched the GS-500, which Ibanez built and Roland loaded with the most incredible electronics that controlled a separate synth unit. The trick was to get the pickup accurate enough to work with guitar strings and trigger the synth. Then ten years later, in the '80s, Roland reattempted releasing a guitar synth with the G-707, a real "Jetsons"-looking futuristic guitar. All of the sounds were in the guitar itself and could be edited and resaved. Cool idea, but it became very impractical for the guitarist at large. Finally in the '90s, Roland was able to develop a pickup system, the GK series, which was very accurate and was able to be mounted universally on guitars.

Roland GK-3 Guitar Pickup—Close-Up

Roland GK-3 Guitar Pickup Mounted on Les Paul

Roland GK-3 Guitar Pickup System

Roland GK-3 Guitar Pickup Mounted on Strat

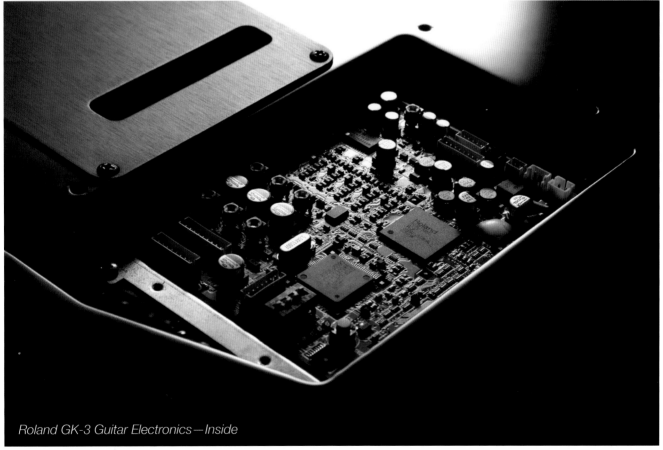

Roland GK-3 Guitar Electronics—Inside

Sadowsky

Guitar master luthier Roger Sadowsky specialized in modifying Fender basses, altering the pickup electronics and replacing it with active electronics with a preamp. In the late 1970s, he opened up his small manufacturing shop in New York City and started making basses for NYC session players like Will Lee and Chuck Loeb. He moved into making guitars and makes a series of hollow bodies and solid bodies. Bass phenomena Tal Wilkenfeld endorses Sadowsky instruments now, and Roger has moved up the ranks and is acknowledged as a prestigious luthier.

Jazz Shredder Chuck Loeb with His Sadowsky Guitar

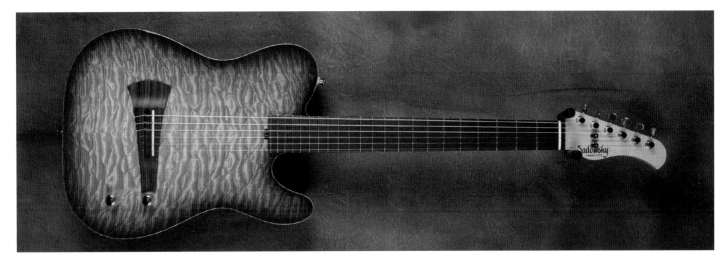

Sadowsky Electric Nylon 6-String Model

Sadowsky Standard T-Style Model

Sadowsky Standard S-Style Model

Sadowsky Vintage S-Style Model

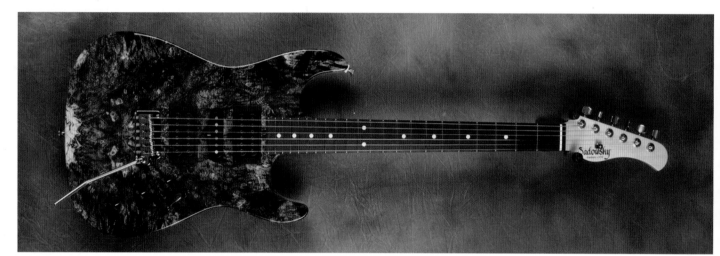

Sadowsky Standard S-Style Model-Brown Marble

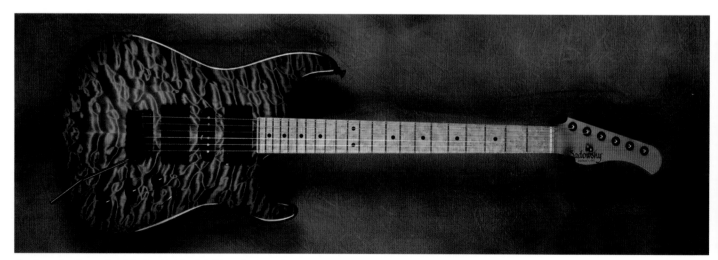

Sadowsky Standard S-Style Model-Blue Quilted Top

Sadowsky Semihollow Body Model

Sadowsky Will Lee Bass Model

Sadowsky Vintage P/J 24 Fret Bass

Sadowsky 5-String Bass 24-Fret Bass

Sadowsky Standard 5-String Bass

Schecter

Schecter actually started out as an aftermarket guitar parts supplier, and I personally remember going down to Rudy's music in New York City and browsing through the various guitar parts. Eventually in the 1980s, it moved into guitar manufacturing, and Pete Townsend was one of the first to endorse it. It has always been known to remake Strats and Teles in different variations. While it never reinvented the wheel, it remained a source for players to buy more affordable guitars. Today, it is very popular among the metal crowd and has an array of young rocker endorsees and even a few familiar ones like Nikki Sixx, Prince, the Cure, and my shredding buddy Chris Poland.

Schecter Hellraiser Strat

Schecter Stargazer 12-String Guitar

Chris Poland Tearing It Up on His Schecter 6-String Guitar

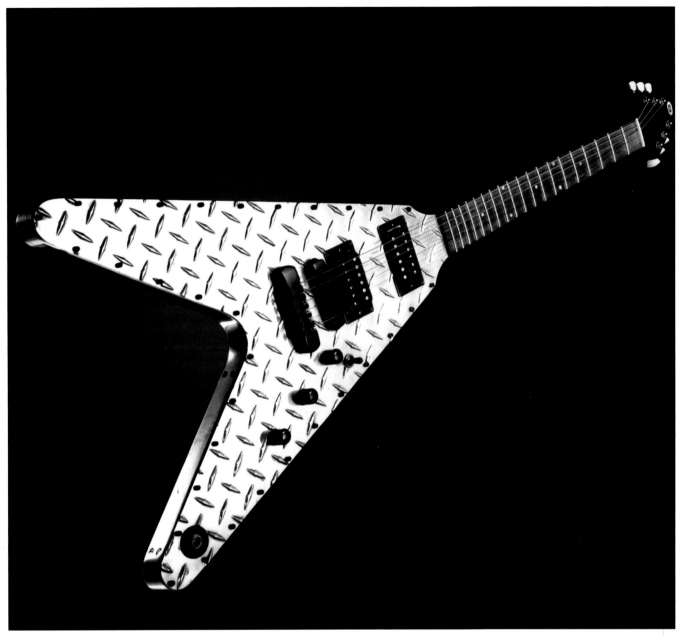

Specimen Aluminum Flying A Model

Specimen

If you think that the day of handcrafted guitars has gone out with the Dodo bird, think again! There is an old-school manufacturer tucked away in Chicago, Illinois. You may not have heard of it, but it still handcrafts guitars the old-fashioned way through carving wood and rasping to hone the guitar into shape. Its medium is not only wood but also other nontraditional materials, such as aluminum, bell brass, and masonite. It was born from the hands of Memphis College student Ian Schneller, who used the term Specimen Products as a name for his sculptures back in 1981. Ian agreed to let me pick his brain in an interview for this book.

Specimen Freeman Royale Hollow Body Model

Can you give us a little background on yourself and how you got started with guitar building and why you started making custom guitars?

After finishing a BFA at the Memphis College of Art in 1984 and an MFA in sculpture at the School of the Art Institute of Chicago in 1986, for some inexplicable reason I began making stringed instruments. This, of course, exiled me from the art world, as utilitarian undertakings are usually verboten in the art setting. I immersed myself in the craft of luthiery, never thinking of it as being any different than art. I find the rich history, traditions, and unforgiving discipline of the stringed instrument geometry very refreshing.

Perhaps the main reason I started making guitars was that I played in a band and could not afford a nice vintage guitar. I had made things all my life, so why not give it a go? It then became a passion.

It seems that in the world of CNC manufacturing, the art of the guitar luthier is lost. How did you come up with the unique designs and what makes your guitars so different?

What makes my Specimens so different from production guitars is the fact that they are all individuals built to exacting geometry from materials that have usually been aged for over a decade. This makes them far more stable than instruments made hastily from young materials. They are also sensible designs. Often they look wild, but I usually adhere to very traditional tenets of construction. I use nonadjustable neck reinforcements, pay special attention to the neck/body join, and take measures to avoid the dreaded skateboard ramp so prevalent in production instruments.

I want my instruments to far outlast me. Servicing instruments for the past twenty-five

Specimen Super Luddite

Specimen Super Luddite—Body

years, I am intimately acquainted with the failure modes of popular models. My instruments are a remedy.

CNC is generally considered flawless, and it is very impressive, but generalizations must be made and tolerances relaxed in order to maintain flow in a production setting, especially when using fickle materials. This equates to built-in slop. There are those who would argue with me, but they would be wrong.

What is the most challenging thing about making your guitars?

The most challenging thing about making my guitars is maintaining a profit margin without having to charge exorbitant prices. Making things properly out of quality materials is time-consuming and expensive. Luckily, the mentality that compares everything to a Stratocaster has broadened a little bit. Independent builders are not considered such anomalies anymore.

Specimen Electric Tiple

contexts, but always try to find new ground. I have little interest in remanifesting historic renditions. I want to create the unseen and unexplored.

The right wood is old wood. The older, the better. I tell all my students to buy as much wood as they can right now and squirrel it away. Buy wood instead of groceries. Ten years goes by very quickly. Then you have something. There is not much good wood left. We have to build with what we have on hand, so be strategic.

I finish with nitrocellulose. As far as I am concerned, it is the only finish suitable for a long-lived instrument because it is serviceable. At some point, shellac/French polish will become the only practical finish due to availability.

There seems to be a debate about the finishes—nitro vs. poly. What is the difference and how does it affect the tone of the instrument?

I don't think poly finishes sound bad if applied sensibly (thinly). It's just that they are all wrong. They feel wrong. They smell wrong. They are not repairable. They are ugly. The same can be said of the water-based lacquers. Nasty.

Do you wind your own pickups or use third party and how important are the electronics in your guitars?

The electronics are as important as anything else. I really like Lindy Fralin's stuff. I machine my own bobbins, and he winds them up the way I like them. This completely liberates me to create my own formats, step off the beaten path when appropriate, and still have great sounding pickups. My electric ukes, mandolins, and tiples are examples. I also use DiMarzio pickups. They are good honest pickups backed up with decent engineering specs. They also have fancy-colored bobbins!

Can you take us through your process of building, from choosing the right wood to the paint finishing?

My process of building starts on the drawing board. I often reference history for dimensions and

Specimen Electric Lute

Specimen Super Luddite—Body

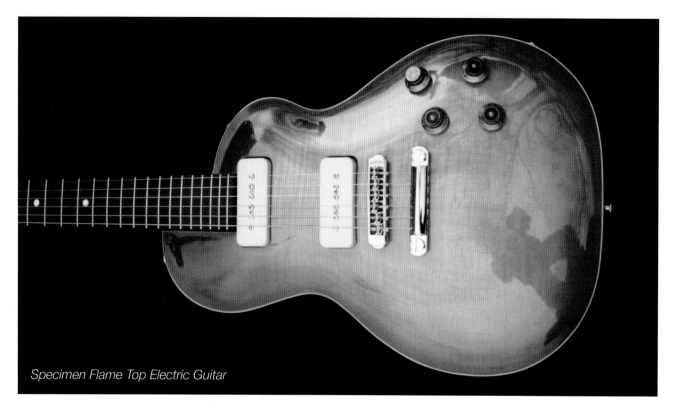

Specimen Flame Top Electric Guitar

Steinberger

This is the case where timing is everything. Like with Ken Parker, Ned Steinberger had a unique vision in guitar building; in fact, you can say that Ned's was more radical than Parker's. First off, Steinberger guitars had no headstock at all and were tuned at the bridge. Secondly, the early models really didn't resemble guitars; they were just sticks with little rectangular bodies. On top of that, they were made of resins and carbon fiber materials with a very cold-feeling fretboard. But they proved to be a winner, especially in the 1980s, where futurism was embraced and an emotion of modernism was in the air. Players like Geddy Lee, Eddie Van Halen, and Allan Holdsworth embraced the guitars. Later, Ned came out with a model that had an actual double cutaway Strat-like body, and he invented a vibrato system that detuned all the strings equally as you pressed the whammy bar.

Steinberger Demon Model

Steinberger Demon Model—Body

Steinberger Synapse Bass—Body

Steinberger Synapse Model

Steinberger Synapse Bass—Neck

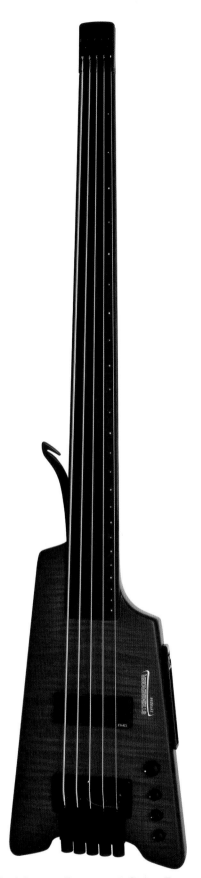

Steinberger Synapse 5-String Bass

Steinberger ZT3 Guitar

Steinberger ZT3 Guitar—Body

Steinberger ZT3 Blue Guitar—Body

Steinberger Synbass 5-String

Steinberger GT Pro 6-String Guitar

Guitar Designers • 207

Tobias

The company originally started in Florida in the late 1970s by Michael Tobias was called The Guitar Shop. After moving to California, Tobias continued to make guitars, including a small run of mahogany Les Paul Junior-styled neck thru designs. Michael was most notably known for his neck thru bass designs with an asymmetrical neck, whereby the neck is thinner on the lower side than the upper side. As business grew and the demands went up for builds, Tobias found it hard to keep up. So in 1990, Michael sold the business to Gibson guitars and moved to the Catskill region of New York, where he started building new guitar designs.

Tobias Growler Bass—Body

Tobias Growler Bass—Back

Tobias Growler Bass

Tom Anderson

Tom Anderson was an employee of the Schecter guitar repair shop in Van Nuys, California, in the '70s. By 1980, he decided to open a boutique custom build shop of his own. Like many other builders at the time, Tom was offering a service that the large manufacturers weren't, the hot rodded Fender Strat. Like PRS, Anderson would design sleek, beautiful quilt-top instruments for players with a high price tag. Initially, his shop was in his garage, but by 1990, Anderson had secured a factory for all of his manufacturing. Today Anderson guitars have such endorsers as Kirk Hammett, Mick Jagger, Neal Schon, and Vivian Campbell.

Tom Anderson Bulldog Maple Carved Flametop

Vox Virage II Hollow Body Model

Vox

At first, in the mid-1950s Vox was an amplifier builder known for its AC15 and AC30 amps. But by 1960, it developed five new guitars in its lineup: the Ace, Duotone, Soloist, Clubman, and Stroller, along with a three-pickup Consort and a two-pickup Escort. It also produced two bass guitars that year, the Contour and Bassmaster. However, they were outsourced and not manufactured by Vox but by Stuart Darkins and Co., a known furniture maker of the time. But by the early '60s Vox came up with a design that would signify the change that was going on in that decade: the Phantom. They looked similar to a lute and were built from the ground up by Vox in their factory. Who could forget The Rolling Stones' guitarist Brian Jones playing a Phantom on the *Ed Sullivan Show* in the mid-sixties? Vox has reincarnated the Phantom in its new model the Apache, with a similar shape and design.

Vox Virage Hollow Body Model

Vox Series 22 Double Cutaway Model

Vox Apache Guitar

Vox Apache Bass Guitar

Warmoth

Similar to the early days of Carvin, Warmoth was a guitar parts company. Warmoth began building replacement necks for Fender guitars. It now sells bodies, necks, and all hardware, including pickups, for customers to assemble their own guitars made from its parts. It cannot sell assembled guitars due to its licensing agreement with Fender. It's also important to note that it is the largest manufacturer of these components in the United States. Other parts companies simply import their parts from other countries. Warmoth actually builds its parts in their Puyallup, Washington, factory. It has supplied necks to Yamaha (900 Series Pacifica) necks and bodies to Valley Arts (Custom Pro Series) and Sadowsky Guitars. The guitars pictured in this section are all made from Warmoth parts and were built by Robert Carter at Warmoth.

Purple Quilted Strat Built by Robert Carter at Warmoth

Quilted Top Les Paul Built by Robert Carter at Warmoth

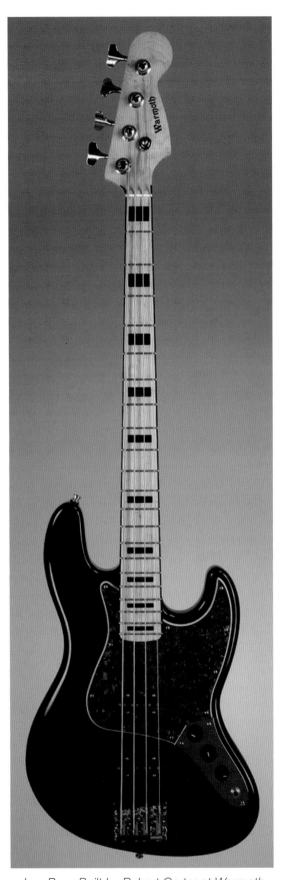

Jazz Bass Built by Robert Carter at Warmoth

Purple Tele Built by Robert Carter at Warmoth

Purple Tele Back Built by Robert Carter at Warmoth

Bengal 5-String Bass Built by Robert Carter at Warmoth

Super Tele Built by Robert Carter at Warmoth

Super Strat Built by Robert Carter at Warmoth

Warwick

In 1982, at age twenty-four, Hans-Peter Wilfer founded the Warwick Company in Bavaria. His father, Fred Wilfer, had founded the European guitar manufacturer Framus in 1946, so young Hans grew up with the family business in his blood. They actually have a showroom in the East Village of Manhattan in the United States with a selection of more than ninety standard and custom shop instruments, plus the complete amplification range from both Warwick and Framus. They even broke the Asian trade barrier and have a custom showroom in Shanghai, China. Warwick started with three different models in the early '80s and now has more than forty different bass guitars in production.

Warwick Corvette 4-String Bass

Warwick Streamer 5-String Bass   *Warwick Dolphin Pro 5-String Bass*

Washburn

George Washburn Lyon founded the company in the 1880s as an acoustic guitar company, which was manufactured by the Lyon & Healy Company. The company went through various incarnations of the name Washburn and a series of owners, eventually landing on its feet in the late 1970s. By taking advantage of the low manufacturing costs in Japan, it was able to sell its guitars cheaply to American musicians. As we've seen with other manufacturers at this time, it cashed in on the Super Strat design along with the Flying V and the semihollow body guitars à la ES 335. In the '90s, Washburn really was cooking with signature models for Nuno Bettencourt, Paul Stanley, and its crown jewel model for Dimebag Darrell. Washburn continues to forge ahead with a plethora of guitar, bass, acoustic, banjo, and even mandolin models.

Washburn N4 Koa Strat Model

Washburn N4 Koa Strat Model—Body

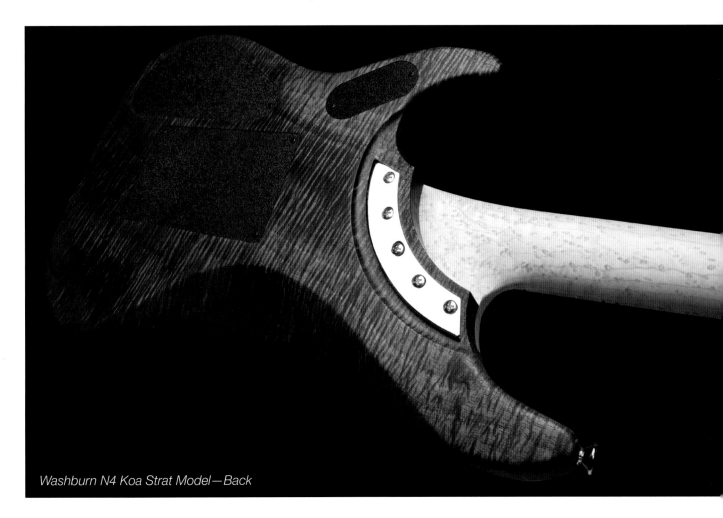

Washburn N4 Koa Strat Model—Back

Washburn J600 Jazz Hollow Body Model   *Washburn J3 Jazz Hollow Body Model*

Washburn N2 Tattoo Model

Washburn HB15 Jazz Hollow Body Model

Washburn HB15C Jazz Hollow Body Model   *Washburn HB36 Semi Hollow Body Model*

Washburn XM-STD Strat

Washburn T24 4-String Bass

Washburn PSV2200 Paul Stanley Flying V

Washburn PSAV Paul Stanley Flying V

Washburn PSV2012 Paul Stanley Guitar

World's Best Bass Player Billy Sheehan Playing His Yamaha Signature Bass Attitude

Billy Sheehan Shredding on His Awesome Double Neck Yamaha Bass

Yamaha

Today Yamaha seems to be an enormous branded corporation making quads, motorcycles, and snowmobiles, not to mention a plethora of musical instruments. But it actually started out as a piano builder in the nineteenth century under the name Nippon Gakki Company. It first started building classical guitars in the early 1940s, but was sidetracked because of reconstruction after WWII and didn't offer an electric guitar until the mid-'60s. But like many of its Japanese contemporaries, it just replicated the large American guitars of Fender and Gibson. It wasn't until the '70s when it received the ultimate endorsement from Carlos Santana for its double cutaway SG-2000. As it moved into the '80s, so did its guitars, designing Super Strats of the day with scalloped necks and dive-bombing whammy bars. One of its more successful guitars is the Attitude bass, designed and played by Billy Sheehan, bass player extraordinaire. Like other guitar manufacturers, Yamaha has grown exponentially through the years and carries a huge assortment of axes that are exported worldwide.

Yamaha BB615 5-String Bass

Yamaha BB Series 4-String Bass

Yamaha RGX520FZ Double Cutaway Guitar

Zemaitis

Tony Zemaitis was a true builder and craftsman who brought a unique artistic design to the guitar that no other luthier has yet achieved. In the 1970s, Tony placed a metal sheet on top of the guitar to avoid feedback from the pickups. He hired gun engraver Danny O'Brien to etch out beautiful designs on the metal top of the guitar, and he was off and running selling to the rich and famous. One of his most valued customers was Ron Wood from the Jeff Beck Group, as well as the Faces, and The Rolling Stones. Eric Clapton, Keith Richards, Ronnie Lane, and George Harrison also owned his gorgeous creations. His guitars represented the lavish rock star life of '70s bands and have reached pinnacle value since his death in 2002.

Zemaitis Sabre Model

Zemaitis Ring Model

Zemaitis Chess Model

Zemaitis Macabre Model

Zemaitis MF501 with Metal Top

Zemaitis SU301 with Dragon Inlay on Top   *Zemaitis SU300 with Diamond Inlay on Top*

Chris Poland – Afterword

I was honored to be asked by Brian to write the afterword to this book about the guitar. First off, I have always been drawn to the instrument and no other. I just love the looks of the guitar. I am a "one-guitar player"—meaning I find the one I love and stick with it.

I must admit I am a "type A" person, and it has trickled down into my passion for playing guitar. I will leave the house at 9:00 p.m., drive to my studio, and play the guitar for five or six hours straight at the drop of a hat. I am driven to do it, and I cannot help myself.

I bet most guitarists who turn your head when you hear them play are driven to it by something almost out of their control. There are a lot of factors that enter into a player's progress, but first and foremost I believe it is their love of music. Emotions play heavily into the gift of guitar playing be it anger, heartbreak, loss, or a sense to prove one's self. Some players play for the fringe benefits. I feel these players never seem to last and are driven by something that is fleeting and not from the heart.

If your heart is not in it, how can you move forward as a player?

I don't judge anyone's reason for playing. Again, it's the fact we as guitarists are driven to do it, be it for the money, fame, and all that goes with it, or the satisfaction a player gets when he, or she, knows that they nailed a solo, or song. Playing the guitar is very rewarding any way you look at it.

That leads me to one thing I feel nonplayers may never experience the same way guitarists do. On a good night I sometimes feel out of body when I am completely in the moment. I have talked to other players about this, and some call it "being in the zone." Whatever that place is—when we are lucky enough to get there—it is worth all the hours invested in practicing. Going to shows as a spectator I have felt this type of energy and/or feeling that a great band can generate. However, when you're playing guitar and this surreal experience happens it is much more intense from the player's perspective, at least for me.

It's hard to describe this, but I guess it's that point when the world drops away and you and the guitar are one. Another great thing about guitar is when we play we each have a sound or touch that is unique, not unlike a fingerprint.

I've always found this very interesting. For example, let's say you have a Strat and a Twin Reverb. Line up five guitar players, and each one will sound totally different than the last—even with identical settings all the way around.

We all have our own voice on guitar. It just takes some time finding it, and the search is the most fun part of it all.

— Chris Poland

Chris Poland Shredding to Live!
Photo credit Mike Sherry

Appendix A Guitar Manufacturers

1. Alembic: *www.alembic.com*
2. B. C. Rich: *www.bcrich.com*
3. Carvin: *www.carvinguitars.com*
4. Charvel: *www.charvel.com*
5. Danelectro: *www.danelectro.com*
6. Dean: *www.deanguitars.com*
7. Eastman: *www.eastmanguitars.com*
8. Eastwood Guitars: *www.eastwoodguitars.com*
9. Ed Roman: *www.edroman.com*
10. Epiphone: *www.epiphone.com*
11. ESP: *www.espguitars.com*
12. Fender: *www.fender.com*
13. Fernandes: *www.fernandesguitars.com*
14. Gander Guitars: *www.ganderguitars.com*
15. Gibson Guitars: *www.gibson.com*
16. Godin: *www.godinguitars.com*
17. Gretsch: *www.gretsch.com*
18. Hagström: *www.hagstromguitars.eu*
19. Hamer: *www.hamerguitars.com*
20. Höfner: *www.hofner.com*
21. Ibanez: *www.ibanez.com*
22. Jackson: *www.jacksonguitars.com*
23. Jay Turser: *www.jayturser.com*
24. Kramer: *www.kramerguitars.com*
25. Music Man: *www.music-man.com*
26. Parker: *www.parkerguitars.com*
27. PRS: *www.prsguitars.com*
28. Rickenbacker: *www.rickenbacker.com*
29. Roland: *www.rolandus.com*
30. Sadowsky: *www.sadowsky.com*
31. Schecter: *www.schecterguitars.com*
32. Speciman: *www.specimenproducts.com*
33. Steinberger: *www.steinberger.com*
34. Tobias: *www.mtdbass.com*
35. Tom Anderson: *www.andersonguitars.com*
36. Vox: *www.voxamps.com/guitars*
37. Warmoth: *www.warmoth.com*
38. Warwick: *www.warwick.de*
39. Washburn: *www.washburn.com*
40. Yamaha: *usa.yamaha.com*
41. Zemaitis: *www.zemaitis-guitars.com*

Appendix B
Guitar Pickups

Seymour Duncan Blackout Single AS-1

The Blackout Single AS-1 will kick your butt, if you dare! I've always been a double humbucker guy, particularly with Gibson guitars. But finally there is a pickup that has a hot output! It reminds me a little of the Eric Clapton preamp system, without the separate preamp. The AS-1 runs on an active circuitry and has a nine-volt battery. Run it through a high-distortion amp, and it really shines with saturation. I have an old Mesa Boogie 50-caliber amp head and ran it through a Legacy 4x12, and it sounded amazing! It retains the single-coil tone but with so much more output. This is the way a Strat should sound. And of course, when backed off on the volume on the guitar, the output cleans up. Just the way I like it, loud and proud, none of this antiquity stuff for me.

Seymour Duncan Pearly Gates SH-PG1 and TBPG-1

Do you like pinch harmonics and Billy Gibbons? Well, this is the pickup that gets it right on the money. It has beautiful tone for the taking. Think of a stock Gibson '59 humbucker with more output. You can really hear the fingers on the fretboard from this pickup. Years ago, I was recording a track for a film called *The Watcher* with Keanu Reeves, and they wanted a ZZ Top track for a scene.

So I had an '83 Kramer Striker in my guitar arsenal loaded with Pearly Gates in the bridge position. I went into the studio and cut the "Tush" soundalike track and really nailed that Billy Gibbons tone, pinch harmonics and all. Needless to say, the producers loved the track, and it made the film. Thank God for those Pearly Gates!

Seymour Duncan Seth Lover Model SH-55

Who in the heck is Seth Lover? Well, let me drop some knowledge on you! While working at the Gibson factory in 1955, Seth invented the humbucker picks, PAF (patent applied for). Before the humbucker invention, everyone was forced to deal with the inherent 60-cycle hum in single-coil pickups. Lover wired two coils electrically out of phase and with reversed magnetic polarities, which canceled the hum before it reached the amp, hence bucking that hum. It was one of the best inventions in history for the electric guitar! So Seymour Duncan and Seth Lover jointly designed this pickup, with a bit of a microphonic tone because the cover is not waxed potted. This is a very vintage-sounding pickup and great for a nice clean tone.

Fender Custom Shop Texas Special

Think of the late great Stevie Ray Vaughan. This is the best replication for his tone, with a midrange chirp, crystal highs, and tight bass along with increased output. They use the alnico 5 magnets and enamel-coated magnet wire. The middle pickup is reverse wound/reverse polarity for hum canceling in positions 2 and 4. Excellent though a Marshall JMP series from the '70s, it can even nail the Ritchie Blackmore sound from those delicious Deep Purple days. It reacts great with pedals, especially boost pedals that give off a sweet saturation tone.

Fender Eric Clapton Noiseless System

Here is a very well-balanced set of pickups running on a nine-volt battery with a powerful active midboost (+25 dB) preamp and TBX circuits. It's very versatile, ranging from the crystal bright clean tones of Robert Cray to the massive overdriven tones of Kings X. The push/pull pot that boosts the midrange is quite handy when pushing the preamp and creates a distinct tone. But you will really feel the air move when you push it through a high-gain Marshall amp, such as the JCM 2000. I had a purple Fender Jeff Beck Signature Strat once loaded with these pickups—the best of both artists—and it burned, as the Deep Purple song states!

Gibson Dirty Fingers

I remember when these pickups with attitude debuted more than twenty years ago. As the Gibson literature said back then, it was "the critical union between power and dirt"—and they weren't kidding. These guys shine on a Les Paul Custom and an ES 335. They have bark and a bite to them and a really nice high output for rock tones. But on the other hand, back off of the guitar volume, and you will hear a clear tone.

I've used these pickups on a Gibson ES 355 Lucille model through a Soldano Reverb O Sonic with 4x10s, and it absolutely screamed when I pushed the gain. And by the same token, it cleaned up very nicely when the gain was brought down, giving off a very bluesy tone.

Gibson Mini Humbucker

This is one of my favorite humbuckers of all time. It sounds fantastic. Don't let the "mini" in the name fool you—the Mini Humbucker is awesome, with tone for days! They first arrived on the scene featured in the 1969 Les Paul Deluxe guitar, the first Les Paul production in years. The pickups were also known as New York humbuckers. These pickups fit into the precarved P-90 pickup cavity using an adaptor ring developed by Gibson, which started the standardization of production for U.S.-built Gibsons.

The bridge position can crank it up and sounds best through a nice high-gain amp, pinch harmonics and all! The neck position has such a rich warmth to it for clean jazz tones and octaves. Just back off of the tone control in the neck position, and you'll swear you have an ES-335. When I was a solo artist on Instinct Records back in the day, I used this setup in a 1977 Gibson Les Paul Deluxe Gold Top quite a lot for the jazz albums I was doing at the time.

Gibson P-90

This is a perfect example of a classic high-output single-coil pickup. I tell you, these pickups are like a '59 Chevy truck. There is nothing that needs to be done—perfect as is. I've played a lot of P-90s, but the Gibson ones are the real deal! I played a Les Paul Studio '60s Tribute that came equipped with a pair of Gibson P-90 single-coil pickups, and they were built like a brick house. These stock pickups were hotter than some of the humbuckers I've played. What killer tone, through a Mesa Boogie, but the point is this cheap guitar, as far as Les Pauls go, really kicked ass with these P-90s. The only downside in recording with these guitars is that it is a single coil, so you are going to get hum and buzz that will have to be adjusted during the session—but it'll be well worth it. There are other manufacturers who make humless P-90s, but you lose all of the tone, so it is a tradeoff.

DiMarzio Super Distortion

The early days of companies that offered aftermarket replacement pickups for guitars were nonexistent, and you were stuck with what came with the guitar stock. In the '70s, that all changed with companies like Seymour Duncan and DiMarzio. The Super Distortion was one of the first pickups offered that was a real hybrid PAF that could be easily replaced in guitars. It was a real steroids pickup with heavy sustain and overdrive monster that was an instant favorite among hard-rock shredders in the '80s. Ace Frehley of Kiss comes to mind, as well as the maestro himself, Steve Vai. Those low-string pinch harmonics that you heard in the '80s were all attributed to this pickup. I believe Van Halen had a lot to do with the sound of those days, and since you couldn't buy his pickups, this was a good substitute.

DiMarzio Virtual P-90

These are high-output P-90 pickups, with a nice fullness to them without the muddiness. The two coils being tuned to different frequency ranges and output voltages removes that 60-cycle hum that I spoke about earlier. So you can adjust tone and balance by pole-piece heights, which is a great idea. The higher the pole piece, the louder the signal; based on the string, you can adjust the volume individually. It's perfect for those classic blues tones and clean jazz tones.

I had this in another Les Paul Deluxe and ran it through an Orange amp with awesome results. There was a nice boost in midfrequencies, while the low end had a real punch to it, plus the top strings did not sound brittle.

Using the right amp with the pickup choice is always an important factor. I also used the Mesa Boogie Mark II; the overdrive was very full with these pickups, working perfectly on jazz chords.

Appendix C
Cool Guitar FX

1. DigiTech Whammy

An absolutely over-the-top effect! Surprisingly it is a very useful tool, for certain types of music like rocktronica or hard rock. The whole idea is through the use of the pedal, it can go up to two octaves up or down from the note played. You also have a harmony side of the pedal that can place a two-part harmony up or down an octave for any note played. On top of that, it has the dive bomb effect and the detuned effect, much like a Uni-Vibe. I used it on a few tracks for the new Guitar Masters CD I'm producing with Reb Beach and Gary Hoey, trippy effect! Great for the whammy bar effect on a guitar that doesn't have one, like a classic Les Paul.

2. Maestro Ring Modulator

Built like a brick shithouse from the 1970s. Mine is from 1973 and is the most musical ring modulator ever built. It's a very simple design and user friendly with sliders that control the pitch, modulation, and volume. There are two toggle switches, one controlling the pitch range high or low, and the other controlling the on/off switch. These effects kind of disappeared in the '80s and '90s and have recently made a comeback. However, many of the ring modulators on the market are unusable, like the Moog and Electro Harmonix, because they are so over-the-top and so uncontrollable that it is impossible to use them effectively in a song. Jeff Beck has been using the Maestro Ring Modulator for forty years, is there anything left to be said?

3. MXR EVH Phase 90

Remember those great old Van Halen tunes "Atomic Punk," "And the Cradle Will Rock," and "Unchained"? Well, you got that sound in this pedal and the simplicity of the original Phase 90 having just one speed knob. But with the EVH model you get the choice of the swirly vintage "script logo" tone of the '70s, then with a push of the button also delivers a modern intense phase tone. And no Van Halen product would be complete without the red candy-striped paint job to match Eddie's guitar! I testify it sounds as good as it looks, if not better.

4. MXR Distortion+

Well there is just not enough to say about this pedal. It possesses terrific distortion with clarity and punch. I have an original I bought from Sam Ash on 48th Street back in 1979 and still have the original box. It's all beat up and dirty, but still delivers that classic overdrive tone when I reach for it. What's great about the early MXR products is they were so easy to use containing one or two knobs. The Distortion+ has only two knobs, one for distortion amount and the other output. It's a very articulated overdrive in which you can hear each note on the fretboard, not like that clunky Big Muff pedal by Electro Harmonix. This has been a favorite among Randy Rhoads, Van Halen, and countless other artists from the era.

5. Ibanez Tube King

Again, this is a pedal that is made with a metal construction which is virtually indestructible. This pedal actually has a 12AX7 tube in it with five control knobs, gain, bass, mid, treble, and master volume. I bought this pedal in the '90s and used it for a lot of live shows across the country, and it worked flawlessly. It delivers a more saturated gain without being too muddy like other pedals. The only downside is it's a bit noisy when recording. I remember opening up for George Benson and Kenny G in '99 at the Jones Beach Amphitheater and loving the tone I was getting; in fact, people complimented me for the tone. However, when I brought it in the studio it was so noisy with an irritating hum, which only got worse as you brought up the volume. So it's one of those tools best used live when no one will notice.

6. Electro-Harmonix Mini QTron

It's one of the more useable pedals from Electro Harmonix. Don't get me wrong, I love their stuff, but some effects are so over-the-top that I can't find a practical use for them. I found this pedal great on bass. In fact, I used it a lot on Randy Coven's bass when I was producing his album *Nu School*. Again this is a pedal with simplicity in controls, with three controls, output/drive, Q, and input/mode. Basically it's an envelope filter that acts as a wah pedal, but you adjust the filter setting from low pass, band pass, and high pass. The Q control adjusts the width of the filter and becomes a creative tool to create funky bass parts.

7. Boss Phase Shifter PH-3

This pedal has a lot of personality. You can create lush chorusing tremolo with clean guitar tones. It has a feature called "rise and fall" modes, which allows you to form unidirectional phase. It also has a tap mode that allows you to sync the phase with a selected tempo. I found this exceptionally useful with electronic music being able to create unique guitar tones to funky big beat grooves. The pedal also provides more vintage phasing effects, especially using a nice Strat tone through a Fender Super Reverb amp. The four controls of rate, depth, res, and stage give a decent amount of controls for any type of music.

8. Snarling Dog Mold Spore Wah

This is a monster wah with that *Star Trek* mold spore sound! It has great control as a wah pedal, better than the run-of-the-mill Dunlop pedals, which results in more expression. The wah has three basic sounds: white room (thick and creamy), voodoo (midrange growl), and Shaft (sharp and funky). The mold spore part of the wah is a secret weapon that will knock you out. It is a ring modulator on steroids. There is a frequency tone that can be set with a chickenhead knob on the side of the pedal, and if used with the wah turned on, you have a filter depending on where the wah is set. I have used this countless times when recording the soundtrack band Asphalt Jungle; it's an excellent choice for electronica music. It has become my main wah pedal because of its flexibility on different styles of music, from rock to funk to jazz.

9. Electro-Harmonix Deluxe Memory Man

I remember when they introduced these pedals. Back in the day growing up in New York City, I used to go down to 48th Street and window-shop at all of the guitar stores. There used be an Electro-Harmonix demo store a couple doors down from Manny's, on the other side of the theater. It was a blast to go there and test out the entire pedal line. I remember they had different stations set up with guitars, and you could test various pedals through amps. Of course, one of the pedal highlights was the Memory Man, a cool analog delay. The surge of electronic music in the '90s brought these pedals back to the foreground, and was utilized, in particular, by the overly popular Chemical Brothers. In 1997, when they came out with their big hit "Block Rockin' Beats," I knew I recognized that crazy sound effect—it was none other than the Memory Man! Crank those feedback and delay controls, and you get the unforgettable effect. Well done!

10. Boss Super Octave OC-3

This is a great-sounding octave divider. The three modes provided are the polyphonic octave, a drive mode with distortion, and the original OC-2 mode. Again, when I was producing the Randy Coven CD, I put him through this effect on more than one occasion, and the effect was stunning. The drive mode with distortion is so cool, and you can control the distortion level. It is great on bass solos and when adding different textures in a track. Try using it on a lower-register riff part and then double-tracking it on the higher register of the guitar—really fat! Try a clean-sounding guitar—say, an ES-335—play some jazz riffs, and put the mix lower for the effect, and you will get a very nice effect in the track. The poly octave effect adjusts to play within a specific note range—very handy when tracking single parts.

11. Keeley Time Machine Boost Pedal

I often use this pedal on my Marshall Plexi 100-watt head through a 4x12 cabinet. It produces a terrific response to the tubes and has three distinct era sounds. There are two channels labeled vintage (1966 and 1971 settings) and the modern, which has a warp mode setting. The modern side uses a +23-dB gain dual JFET, which gets into the territory of Mesa Boogie in terms of ultimate overdrive tone machine. What's nice about this pedal is that there is very little coloration to your guitar tone except giving you boost/saturation to your amp tone. I also put it through a Marshall JTM 45, which saturates the tone further but still keeps the natural sound of the amp.

12. Keeley Ibanez Tube Screamer TS808

This is the legendary 808 pedal, but modified by Keeley for outstanding performance. Basically it has the new JRC chip installed in it, as well as the increase of the gain range, meaning it gets cleaner and more distorted through the range of the drive control. Keeley also addresses the limited bass response that cuts so much of the huge midrange bump in the sound. And they modified the tone control, enabling the user to get more bass frequency response.

Aside from all the technical stuff, just plug it in an old Fender Super Reverb and listen to that sweet tone and how improved it sounds from the original. When recording Leslie West, I put him through the Marshall JCM 800 with this pedal, and it was overdrive heaven, catching all of those pinch harmonics.

13. Dunlop Uni-Vibe

Can you say Robin Trower, "Bridge of Sighs"? This is a great reissue of the original, which always had a lot of electrical issues back in the day. It's not just a cheap chorus pedal—it is so much more! The sound has an incredible rotary/Leslie cabinet sounding pedal, boasting hand-matched photoresistors with a long-life incandescent lamp. This is a true Hendrix machine, right from the stages of Woodstock!

I love putting a clean-sounding semihollow-body guitar through it and hearing the distinctiveness of each string in a chord go from one side of the stereo field to the other. When I was producing the track "Tarquinius Maximus" for the compilation *Guitar Masters Vol. 3 & 4: Les Paul Dedication*, I used it on the clean rhythm tracks, and Chris Poland took a solo using this sound as well. Pure mojo!

14. Electro-Harmonix Micro Synth

This is a really sick over-the-top pedal by the effects guru himself, Mike Mathews. It's a very cool effect, and if you're like me, you'd rather play the synth sounds through your guitar than through a keyboard. You can get everything from the classic Moog sounds to new experimental sounds. The pedal has a two-pole analog resonant filter, a four-voice mixer section (suboctave, original, octave up, and square wave), a square wave voice that can be used as a distortion tone, and start/stop filter frequency sliders with adjustable rate for full control over the filter's sweep direction and speed. You can also adjust the attack time control for fading in notes. It's great for experimental electronica music—I have used it on a number of drum and bass tracks I produced on the Asphalt Jungle CD, *Junglization*. This is a fun pedal for a guitar to dig into and get those old analog synth sounds.

Bibliography

1. **Electric Guitars: The Illustrated Encyclopedia** by Tony Bacon, Dave Burrluck, Paul Day, and Michael Wright. Published by Thunder Bay Press

2. **Electric Guitars and Basses; A Photographic History** by George Gruhn and Walter Carter. Published by Backbeat Books

3. **50 Years of the Gibson Les Paul** by Tony Bacon. Published by Backbeat Books

4. **The Ultimate Gibson Book** by Paul Day and Walter Carter. Published by Metro Books

5. **Guitars Illustrated** by Terry Burrows. Published by Billboard Books

6. **The Ibanez Electric Guitar Book** by Tony Bacon. Published by Backbeat Books

7. **The Ultimate Guitar Sourcebook** by Tony Bacon. Published by Race Point Publishing

8. **Classic Guitars** by Walter Carter. Published by Metro Books

9. **Guitar Trivia** by Michael Heatley. Published by Metro Books

10. **Jimi Hendrix Sessions** by John McDermott with Billy Cox and Eddie Kramer. Published by Little, Brown & Company

Guitar Credits

1. Book cover guitars owned by Brian Tarquin

2. **Chapter 1:**
   - Pictures 2, 4, 6-8, 10 guitars owned by Brian Tarquin
   - Pictures 3, 5, 9 guitars Courtesy of Alto Music

3. **Chapter 2:**
   - Picture 7 guitar owned by Brian Tarquin
   - Pictures 1-6, 8 & 9, 24 & 25 guitars Courtesy of Alto Music

4. **Chapter 3:**
   - Pictures 8, 11 guitars owned by Brian Tarquin
   - Pictures 1, 2, 5, 6, 18, 19 guitars Courtesy of Alto Music
   - Picture 20 of Jeff Beck by Ross Halfin

5. **Chapter 4:**
   - Pictures 14, 20-22 guitars owned by Brian Tarquin
   - Pictures 15-19 guitars Courtesy of Alto Music

6. **Chapter 5:**
   - Pictures 2, 10, 12, 15, 16, 24 guitars owned by Brian Tarquin
   - Pictures 19, 20, 24 by guitars Courtesy of Alto Music

7. **Chapter 6:**
   Charvel
   - Pictures 3-5 guitars Courtesy of Alto Music

   Dean
   - Picture 3 guitar owned by Brian Tarquin

   Eastman
   - Picture 1 guitar Courtesy of Alto Music

   Eastwood
   - Picture 1 guitar owned by Brian Tarquin

   ESP
   - Pictures 1-4 guitars Courtesy of Alto Music

   Godin
   - Picture 1 guitar Courtesy of Alto Music

   Gretsch
   - Pictures 1 & 4 guitars Courtesy of Alto Music

   Hamer
   - Picture 1 guitar Courtesy of Alto Music

Hofner
- Picture 1 guitar Courtesy of Alto Music

Ibanez
- Pictures 2-5, 8 guitars owned by Brian Tarquin
- Pictures 6, 7, 9-13 guitars Courtesy of Alto Music

Jackson
- Pictures 1-4 guitars Courtesy of Alto Music

Kramer
- Pictures 1a & 2 guitars owned by Brian Tarquin

PRS
- Pictures 1 & 2 guitars Courtesy of Alto Music

Rickenbacker
- Pictures 1 & 2 guitars Courtesy of Alto Music

Schecter
- Pictures 1 & 2 guitar Courtesy of Alto Music

Yamaha
- Pictures 3-5 by Courtesy of Alto Music

Photography

1. Book cover and author photo photo by Erik Christian

2. **Chapter 1:**
   - Picture 1 Steve Vai Photo Courtesy of Favored Nations Entertainment
   - Pictures 2-9 taken by Erik Christian
   - Picture 10 Brian Tarquin in the late 1990s at Summerfest, Wisconsin

3. **Chapter 2:**
   - Pictures 1-9, 24 & 25 taken by Erik Christian

   - Pictures 10-23, 26-29 Courtesy of Epiphone

4. **Chapter 3:**
   - Pictures 1, 2, 5, 6, 8, 11, 18, 19 by Erik Christian
   - Pictures 3, 4, 7, 9, 10, 12-17, Courtesy of Fender
   - Picture 20 by Ross Halfin

5. **Chapter 4:**
   - Pictures 1-13, 23 Courtesy of Gibson
   - Pictures 14-22 by Erik Christian

6. **Chapter 5:**
   - Pictures 1, 3-9, 11, 13, 14, 17, 18, 21-23, 25 Courtesy of Gibson
   - Pictures 10, 12, 15, 16, 19, 20, 24 by Erik Christian
   - Picture 2 by Geoff Gray at The Iridium

7. **Chapter 7:**
   Alembic
   - Picture 1 Courtesy of Stanley Clarke
   - Pictures 2-8 Courtesy of Alembic

   Carvin
   - Pictures 1-16 Courtesy of Carvin

   Charvel
   - Pictures 1 & 2 Courtesy of Charvel
   - Pictures 3-5 by Erik Christian

   Danelectro
   - Pictures 1-10 Courtesy of Danelectro

   Dean
   - Pictures 1, 2, 4-6 Courtesy of Dean
   - Picture 3 by Erik Christian
   - Picture 7 by Brian Tarquin

   Eastman
   - Picture 1 by Erik Christian

   Eastwood
   - Picture 1 by Erik Christian
   - Pictures 2-15 Courtesy of Eastwood

   Ed Roman
   - Pictures 1-6 Courtesy of Ed Roman

   ESP
   - Pictures 1-4 by Erik Christian

   Fernandes
   - Pictures 1-8 Courtesy of Fernandes

Gander
- Pictures 1-6 Courtesy of Gander

Godin
- Picture 1 by Erik Christian

Gretsch
- Pictures 1 & 4 by Erik Christian
- Pictures 2 & 3 Courtesy of Gretsch

Hagstrom
- Pictures 1-9 Courtesy of Hagström

Hamer
- Picture 1 by Erik Christian
- Pictures 2 & 3 Courtesy of Hamer

Hofner
- Picture 1 by Erik Christian

Ibanez
- Picture 1 Courtesy of Joe Satriani
- Pictures 2-13 by Erik Christian

Jackson
- Pictures 1-4 by Erik Christian

Jay Turser
- Pictures 1-19 Courtesy of Jay Turser

Kramer
- Picture 1 Eddie Van Halen by David Plastik
- Pictures 1a & 2 by Erik Christian
- Pictures 3-21 Courtesy of Gibson

Music Man
- Picture 1 Courtesy of Steve Morse
- Pictures 2-4 Courtesy of Music Man

Parker
• Pictures 1-10 Courtesy of Parker

PRS
• Pictures 1 & 2 by Erik Christian
• Picture 3 Courtesy of Denny Jiosa

Rickenbacker
• Pictures 1 & 2 by Erik Christian

Roland
• Pictures 1-7 Courtesy of Roland

Sadowsky
• Picture 1 Courtesy of Chuck Loeb
• Pictures 2-12 Courtesy of Sadowsky

Schecter
• Pictures 1 & 2 by Erik Christian

Specimen
• Pictures 1-8 Courtesy of Specimen

Steinberger
• Pictures 1-11 Courtesy of Gibson

Tobias
• Pictures 1-3 Courtesy of Gibson

Tom Anderson
• Picture 1 Courtesy of Tom Anderson

Vox
• Pictures 1-5 Courtesy of Vox

Warmoth
• Pictures 1-8 Courtesy of Rob Carter

Warwick
• Pictures 1-3 Courtesy of Warwick

Washburn
• Pictures 1-14 Courtesy of Washburn

Yamaha
• Pictures 1 & 2 Courtesy of Billy Sheehan Productions
• Pictures 3-5 by Erik Christian

Zemaitis
• Pictures 1-7 Courtesy of Zemaitis

Index

Charvel 17, 99-101, 153, 237, 247, 249
Christian, Charlie 15, 55
Clapton, Eric 41, 42, 44, 231, 238, 239
Clarke, Stanley 82, 249
CNC manufacturing 43, 118, 133
Cobain, Kurt 44, 45

D
Danelectro Company 15, 102
Daniel, Nathan 15, 102
Darrell, Dimebag 220
Dean guitars 106, 237, 247
Diddley, Box
DiMarzio pickups 134, 201, 240
Direct Mounting 120, 122
Direct Tonal Transfer 120

E
Eastman guitars 109, 237, 247, 249
Eastwood Guitars 109-116, 237, 247, 249
Ed Roman Guitars 117-122, 237, 249
Epiphone 14, 15, 21-37, 39, 67, 102, 146, 237, 248
    Broadway (Masterbilt series) 23, 31
    Casino 25, 28, 36
    Triumph (Masterbilt series) 23
ESP guitars (Electric Sound Products) 16, 17, 41, 123-125, 237, 247, 249
    Kamikaze 123
    LTD brand 123-125

F
Fender 13, 16-19, 39- 51, 67, 71, 90, 126, 133, 145, 146, 176, 185, 190, 210, 214, 229, 237, 239, 242, 244, 248
    Broadcaster 40, 67
    Esquire 16, 40
    Jaguar 41, 44
    Jazzmaster 40, 41
    Mustang 41, 44, 45
    Stratocaster 16, 40, 200

Fender Custom Shop 42, 43, 239
    Artist Signature Series 16, 41, 239
Fender, Leo 13, 16, 39-41, 43, 45, 47, 176
Fernandes Guitars 126-129, 237, 249
    Sustainer 126
Fishman, Larry 179
Floyd Rose tremolo 17, 164, 167, 168, 170
Ford, Mary 70, 73
Fralin, Lindy (pickups) 201
Frehley, Ace 52, 75, 76, 240

G
Gambale, Frank 90
Gander Guitars 130-132, 237, 249
    Libra 130
Gander, Ray (luthier) 130
Gibbons, Billy 238, 239
Gibson guitars 13, 15-18, 23, 25, 39, 52-79, 85, 106, 126, 133, 144, 145, 146, 184, 185, 208, 229, 237, 238-240, 245, 248-250
    Double Neck Electric Hawaiian 56
    EH-150 56
    ES-150 15, 55, 56
    ES-335 57, 62, 220, 239, 240, 243
    Explorer 28, 60, 61, 144, 146
    Flying V 17, 59-61, 106, 144, 153, 154, 175, 220, 226
    L-5 16, 23, 55,
    Les Paul Deluxe 73, 240
Gibson, Orville (luthier) 13, 53, 55, 57, 58
GK-2A Divided Pickup 18, 19
Godin Guitars 134, 135, 237, 247, 249
Godin, Robert 134
Gray, Geoff (*Far & Away Studios*) 67, 68, 70, 249
Gretsch, Friedrich 135
Gretsch guitars 15, 41, 135-137, 237, 247, 249
    White Falcon 135
Guitar Player Magazine 106, 155

R

Rhoads, Randy 153, 242
Richards, Keith 25, 176, 231
Rickenbacker 13, 14, 23, 39, 185, 237,
    247, 250
Rickenbacker, Adolph 13
Rico, Bernardo "Bernie" Chavez 85
Robinson, Mike 109
Roland Synth Guitar series 18, 19,
    186, 187
    G-707 18, 187
    GK-2A 18, 19
    GS-500 187
Rolling Stones, The 25, 123, 211
Roman, Ed (luthier) 117-122, 249
    Quicksilver 120
Ro-Pat-In 14

S

Sam Ash (48th Street, NYC) 17, 41, 85, 242
Sadowsky Guitars 190-194, 214, 237, 250
Sadowsky, Roger (luthier) 190
Santana, Carlos 18, 184, 229
Satriani, Joe 16, 146, 249
Schecter guitars 17, 41, 123, 195, 196, 210, 237,
    247, 250
Schneller, Ian 197
Schon, Neal 164, 210
Seymour Duncan 42, 52, 73, 74, 76, 134, 148,
    150, 164, 238, 239, 240
Sheehan, Billy 229
Smith, Paul Reed (luthier) 18, 184, 185
Specimen Products 197-202, 237, 250
Stanley, Paul 146, 220
Stathopoulo, Epaminondas "Epi" 14,
    21-13, 25
Stathopoulo, Anastasios 14, 21
Steinberger 203-207, 237, 250
Steinberger, Ned 203
Stromberg Electro 14

T

Tarquin, Brian 19, 43, 246-249
Tobias 208. 209, 237, 250
Tom Anderson Guitars 210, 237, 250
Townsend, Pete 195
Turser, Jay 155-163, 249

U

Ultimate Guitar Works 134

V

Vai, Steve 13, 16, 90, 99, 146, 153, 240, 248
Van Halen, Eddie 17, 49, 99, 146,153, 164-166,
    176, 203, 240, 242, 249
Vaughan, Stevie Ray 41, 44, 49, 239
Vox 211-213, 237, 250
    Apache 211, 213
    Phantom 211

W

Walker, Tom 176
Warmoth 214-217, 237, 250
Warwick Company 218, 219, 237, 250
Washburn Guitars 17, 220-227, 237, 250
    Corvette 218
    N2 Tattoo 223
Wickersham, Ron and Susan 82
Wilfer, Hans-Peter 218
Wilkenfeld, Tal 190
White, Forrest 176
Wood, Ron 231
Wylde, Zakk 20, 25, 33, 35, 65

Y

Yamaha 17, 133, 214, 228-230, 237, 247, 250
    Attitude bass 228, 229
    SG-2000 229

Z

Dean 106-108, 237, 247, 249
Zemaitis 231-234, 237, 250

**Books
from
Allworth
Press**

Booking Performance Tours: Marketing and Acquiring Live Arts and Entertainment
by Tony Micocci (paperback, 6 x 9, 304 pages, $24.95)

How to Grow as a Musician: What All Musicians Must Know to Succeed
by Sheila E. Anderson (paperback, 6 x 9, 256 pages, $25.50)

Making and Marketing Music: The Musician's Guide to Financing, Distributing, and Promoting Albums
by Jodi Summers (paperback, 6 x 9, 240 pages, $19.95)

Making it in the Music Business
by Lee Wilson (paperback, 6 x 9, 256 pages, $24.95)

Managing Artists in Pop Music: What Every Artist and Manager Must Know to Succeed
by Mitch Weiss and Perri Gaffney (paperback, 6 x 9, 288 pages, $23.95)

Profiting from Your Music and Sound Project Studio
by Jeffrey Fisher (paperback, 6 x 9, 224 pages, $24.95)

The Quotable Musician: From Bach to Tupac
by Sheila E. Anderson (paperback, 7.6 x 7.6, 224 pages, $19.95)

Rock Star 101: A Rock Star's Guide to Survival and Success in the Music Business
by Marc Ferrari (paperback, 176 pages, $17.95)

The Songwriter's and Musician's Guide to Nashville
by Sherry Bond (paperback, 6 x 9, 256 pages, $19.95)

Starting Your Career as a Musician
by Neil Tortorella (paperback, 6 x 9, 240 pages, $19.95)

Insider's Guide to Music Licensing
by Brian Tarquin (paperback, 6 x 9, 256 pages, $19.95)

To see our complete catalog or to order online, please visit *www.allworth.com.*